re the last time s

The Official Book of
The Scottish Terrier

TS-213

Distributed in the UNITED STATES to the Pet Trade by T.F.H. Publications, Inc., One T.F.H. Plaza, Neptune City, NJ 07753; distributed in the UNITED STATES to the Bookstore and Library Trade by National Book Network, Inc. 4720 Boston Way, Lanham MD 20706; in CANADA to the Pet Trade by H & L Pet Supplies Inc., 27 Kingston Crescent, Kitchener, Ontario N2B 2T6; Rolf C. Hagen Ltd., 3225 Sartelon Street, Montreal 382 Quebec; in CANADA to the Book Trade by Vanwell Publishing Ltd., 1 Northrup Crescent, St. Catharines, Ontario L2M 6P5 ; in ENGLAND by T.F.H. Publications, PO Box 15, Waterlooville PO7 6BQ; in AUSTRALIA AND THE SOUTH PACIFIC by T.F.H. (Australia), Pty. Ltd., Box 149, Brookvale 2100 N.S.W., Australia; in NEW ZEALAND by Brooklands Aquarium Ltd. 5 McGiven Drive, New Plymouth, RD1 New Zealand; in Japan by T.F.H. Publications, Japan—Jiro Tsuda, 10-12-3 Ohjidai, Sakura, Chiba 285, Japan; in SOUTH AFRICA by Multipet Pty. Ltd., P.O. Box 35347, Northway, 4065, South Africa. Published by T.F.H. Publications, Inc.

MANUFACTURED IN THE UNITED STATES OF AMERICA
BY T.F.H. PUBLICATIONS, INC.

The Official Book of
The Scottish Terrier

by Muriel P. Lee

T.F.H. Publications, Inc., is delighted to publish this breed book for the Scottish Terrier Club of America. Thanks to the cooperation of the STCA which makes this volume possible, a substantial royalty from the sales of this book will be donated to the betterment of the Scottish Terrier across the United States. The publisher also wishes to extend its gratitude to author Muriel Lee for her commitment to the Scottish Terrier breed and her unwavering professionalism as an author.

Andrew De Prisco
Editor

Contents

John Sheehan showing Ch. Firebrand's Sunday Scherzo to BOS at STCA Rotating Specialty in 1983 under judge Dick Hensel.

Dedication

To John Sheehan, best of friends,
and Dick Hensel, sadly missed friend

About the Author

Muriel Lee has been active in the dog world since 1965, when she purchased her first Old English Sheepdog. As they were rather rare

Author Muriel Lee with great Scottie friend John Sheehan.

in those days and difficult to come by, she looked through the local want ads, called a breeder and was told, "Ah, you want the dog with the hair—an Old English Sheepdog—I have Shetland Sheepdogs, which look like a little Collie." Somehow, since those days, she has become knowledgeable enough to write a book about Scottish Terriers!

Four Old English champions later, she decided to find a breed that was less bulky and easier to keep. Having grown up with a Wire Fox Terrier, she found it natural to look at the Terrier group of dogs and eventually settled upon a Scottish Terrier. She purchased her first Scottie from John Sheehan of Firebrand Kennels and told him that it was "a lot cheaper by the pound to buy an Old English Sheepdog than to buy a Scottish Terrier" and left Mr. Sheehan speechless for one of the few times in his life.

Over the years she has shown many Scots and whelped many litters, both for herself and for John Sheehan. Through her whelping experience, she wrote *The Whelping and Rearing of Puppies: A Complete and Practical Guide*, currently in its fourth printing, in addition to *The Dog Breeder's Organizer*. The whelping book, first published in 1984, continues to be the book of choice on whelping by breeders throughout the country.

Muriel was a self-employed businesswoman in Minneapolis for 22 years, owning a drinking and eating establishment just off the University of Minnesota campus. Upon retirement in 1986 she worked at a large metro hospital as a volunteer coordinator for three years and still helps out in the patient relations department when needed.

She is a graduate of the University of Minnesota with a degree in

Muriel Lee with a favorite Scot.

music, is an avid gardener, and a proficient needleworker, having had her original pieces exhibited in Minneapolis, Charleston, Dallas and Monaco, in addition to the AKC "Bitches in Stitches" exhibition in 1982. She has been awarded ribbons nationally and internationally for her needlework.

Her first dog articles were published in *The Bobtail Express,* an Old English Sheepdog magazine published in the early 1970s by Dick Beauchamp. She was the editor for the 1990 Scottish Terrier Club of America's Handbook, which received a nomination for excellence from the Dog Writer's Association of America.

Muriel has been a member of the Minneapolis Kennel Club for 25 years and served as treasurer for 18 years. She is a member of the Lake Minnetonka Kennel Club and has been their chief ring-steward for the summer and winter shows for many years. She is an active member of the STCA and will be editing the 1995 Yearbook and the 2000 Centenary Handbook. She is an AKC-licensed judge of Scottish Terriers and occasionally still shows the Firebrand dogs.

Muriel now lives in a town house with an 11-year-old orange Persian cat who has a champion sire and with a young "Morris" cat who came from the humane society.

Morris assisting in the editorial process.

Introduction

Ah, the Scottish Terrier! The big dog in the little package—the tyke with the short legs and the long head. The dog that has the courage of a German Shepherd and thinks that he is the size of a Great Dane. Perhaps the writer William Haynes said it best: "Words fail me when I want to describe the Scottish Terrier. To me he is the dog of dogs, my personal opinion being: all dogs are good; any terrier is better; a Scottie is BEST! . . . Nobody seems to fall madly in love with a Scottie at first sight, but nobody can live in the same house with him a week and not love him."

This is not a dog for everyone, but those who have had a Scottish Terrier as a comrade will never forget the experience. For many, Scotties will become lifelong companions, and each Scot in the household that goes to his reward is replaced with a new puppy. Indeed, once your heart is given to a Scottish Terrier, it will remain true and steadfast to the breed for a lifetime.

This book will give you an overview of the Scottish Terrier. You should know what the Scottish Terrier was bred for, where it came from and the historical facts that have made this such an enduring breed. You may become interested in showing or breeding your dog, and helpful information will be given for those endeavors. You should know about the temperament of the breed and the care that will be required, as well as any problems that you could expect. But most of all, you will learn what a delight it is to own this marvelous breed and that years of enjoyment will be yours when you make a commitment to the Scottish Terrier.

Ch. Deblin's Back Talk mans the phone. Owned by D. Brookes, "Tony" gets many calls.

11

Ch. Dundee rendered by Edwin Megaree.

Early Development of the Breed

In the history of the dog world the Scottish Terrier is not an ancient breed; however, its official beginnings, which trace back to the late 1800s, place it among one of the older breeds recognized by the American Kennel Club.

The Scottish Terrier belongs to the group of dogs described as terriers, from the Latin word *terra,* meaning earth. The terrier is a dog that has been bred to work beneath the ground to drive out small and large vermin, rodents, and other animals that can be a nuisance to country living.

All of the dogs in the terrier group originated in the British Isles with the exception of the Miniature Schnauzer. Many of the terrier breeds were derived from a similar ancestor and as recently as the mid-1800s, the terriers fell roughly into two basic categories: the rough-coated, short-legged dogs of Scotland, and the longer legged, smooth-coated dogs of England.

The family of Scotch Terriers—those bred in Scotland—divide themselves into the modern Scottish Terrier, the West Highland White Terrier and the Dandie Dinmont Terrier. The Skye Terrier is also considered to be a part of this group. In the early 1800s, dogs referred to as the Scotch Terrier could be any of the first three breeds mentioned. Interbreeding was common among these breeds and all three breed types could come from one litter.

In 1860, the second year of organized dog shows, the types of dogs shown in the class called "Scotch Terriers of all Kinds" had been further divided into the Rough-haired Terrier, the Aberdeen, the Highland and the Skye. In 1879 at the Kennel Club show in London, classes were offered for the first time for the Scotch, or Broken-haired Terrier, and this marks the official beginning for our breed. Thirteen dogs were shown in this class. The two winners, "Tartan" and "Splinter II," were bred and produced a bitch named "Worry." She, in turn, produced four champions and was the granddam of a great champion named "Dundee."

As breeders started exhibiting at dog shows, it was realized that there must be more uniformity within the breed, i.e., all pups in a litter should look alike as well as being of the same type as their sire and dam.

In 1882, a group of Scottish Terrier fanciers from Scotland met and formed a breed club. Although this club had many difficulties and did not survive, these breeders were able to reach some unanimity and initiated the writing and the acceptance of the first breed standard. Some stability as to type was finally brought to the breed.

This first standard is reprinted here in its entirety. Note that the current standard has changed very

13

little since this was written, well over a century ago. The most notable differences are in coat color and size. The breed now is slightly taller and heavier; however, it will be seen that many of the early dogs were apparently of good size! Brindles, blacks and wheatens are acceptable and no color is to be preferred over another.

This standard first appeared in Vero Shaw's *The Illustrated Book of the Dog,* and was drawn up by J. B. Morrison and Mr. Thomson Gray.

GENERAL APPEARANCE—is that of a thick-set, compact, short-coated

Ch. Alister, half-brother to Ch. Dundee, born 1885.

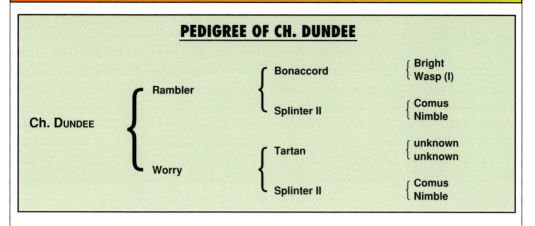

PEDIGREE OF CH. DUNDEE

Ch. DUNDEE
- Rambler
  - Bonaccord
    - Bright
    - Wasp (I)
  - Splinter II
    - Comus
    - Nimble
- Worry
  - Tartan
    - unknown
    - unknown
  - Splinter II
    - Comus
    - Nimble

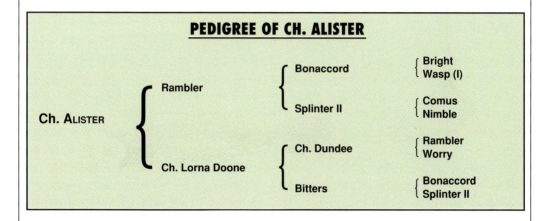

PEDIGREE OF CH. ALISTER

Ch. ALISTER
- Rambler
  - Bonaccord
    - Bright
    - Wasp (I)
  - Splinter II
    - Comus
    - Nimble
- Ch. Lorna Doone
  - Ch. Dundee
    - Rambler
    - Worry
  - Bitters
    - Bonaccord
    - Splinter II

terrier, standing about $9^1/_2$ inches high, with body long in comparison, and averaging 16 pounds or 17 pounds weight for dogs and 2 pounds less for bitches. Ears and tail uncut. Although in reality no higher at shoulder than the Skye or Dandie Dinmont, it has a leggier appearance from the fact that the coat is much shorter than in those two varieties. The head is carried pretty high, showing an intelligent cheery face.

TEMPERAMENT—an incessant restlessness and perpetual motion, accompanied by an eager look, ask- ing plainly for the word of com- mand; a muscular form, fitting him for the most arduous work; and sagacity, intelligence, and courage to make the most of the situation, qualify the Scottish Terrier for the role of "friend of the family," or "companion in arms," in a sense unsurpassed by any other dog, large or small.

HEAD—is longish and bold, and is full between the eyes. It is free from long, soft, or woolly hair and is smaller in the bitch than in the dog.

MUZZLE—is a most important point, and should be long and very powerful, tapering slightly to the nose, which should be well formed, well spread over the muzzle, and black in colour. There must be no approach to snipeyness. The teeth should be perfectly level in front, neither being under nor overshot, fitting well together.

EYES—are small, well sunk in the head, dark hazel, bright and expressive, with heavy eyebrows.

EARS—are very small and free from long hair, feather, or fringe; in fact, as a rule, rather bare of hair and never cut.

NECK—is short, thick, very muscular, well set between the shoulders and showing great power.

CHEST AND BODY—the body gives an impression of great strength, being little else than a combination of bone and muscle. The chest is broad and deep, the ribs flat—a wonderful provision of nature, indispensable to dogs often compelled to force their way through burrows and dunes on their sides. The back broad, the loin thick and very strong. This is a feature calling for special attention, as a dog in any degree weak in hindquarters lacks some of the main features of this breed and should on no account be used as a stud dog. The body is covered with a dense, hard, wet-resisting coat about two inches long.

LEGS—the forelegs are short and straight with immense bone for a dog of this size. Elbows well in and not outside, the forearm particularly muscular. The hind legs are also strong, the thighs being well-developed and thick, the hocks well bent.

FEET—are small and firmly padded to resist the stony ground; nails strong, generally black. Although free from feathering, the legs and feet are well covered with hair to the very toes.

TAIL—should not exceed seven or eight inches, covered with the same quality and length of hair as the body, and is carried with a slight bend, never docked.

COLOUR—various shades of grey, or grizzle, and brindle, the most desirable colour being red brindle with black muzzle and ear-tips.

Of course, the rather colorful and expressive language of the nineteenth century has unfortunately been brought into the confines of the twentieth century.

Breeders in England and Scotland now had a mental picture to draw from of what they should expect to see in their kennel runs. In addition, they were now acquiring good stock to breed from and to breed to. By 1905, reputable breeders were turning out excellent stock with well thought-out breeding programs.

Two dogs are considered to be the first pillars of the breed and if one were to persevere long enough in their search, they would find these two animals in the beginning of almost every Scottish Terrier pedigree. *Ch. Dundee* and *Ch. Alister* form this strong background and their pedigrees are given here for you to compare. Note that Ch. Alister is not only the grandson of Ch. Dundee but also his half-brother, with both dogs being sired by Rambler.

Ch. Dundee, whelped in 1882, was described in early books as a dark brindle dog with a good body and heavy bone, weighing close to 24 pounds. A journalist described his coat as "so hard it might have been borrowed from a hedgehog." He was said to have large but well-placed ears, a clean skull and a very keen expression. He sired only one champion, the dam of Ch. Alister, but became noteworthy as the grandsire of Ch. Rascal, born in 1889, another highly regarded Scot.

Ch. Alister, born in 1885, was one of the first black Scotties to become a notable winner in the ring. Ch. Alister sired many champions, one of which was Ch. Tiree, the first American Scottish Terrier champion.

By 1900, the Scottish Terrier was a well-established breed with many friends and fanciers in the British Isles. The interest in the United States was developing as a small and dedicated group of friends was growing on American shores.

Ch. Dundee, born 1882, was famous for his hard-as-a-hedgehog coat.

Ch. Heather Necessity, whelped 1927.

Ch. Albourne Barty, whelped 1925.

Ch. Heather Ambition, whelped 1932.

Ch. Heather Fashion Hint, whelped 1929.

The Scottish Terrier Scene in Great Britain: 1900 to 1940

The Scottish Terrier has had a legion of admirers, fanciers and breeders in England and it is from this foundation that the American Scots developed. For this reason, a history of the early English dogs should be appreciated.

An individual who contributed immensely to the written history of the breed was Mrs. Dorothy Caspersz. Mrs. Caspersz owned her first Scottie in 1894 and attended her first dog show in 1907. She continued to be vitally active in the breed until her death in 1961. Mrs. Caspersz judged many of the early English winners and has described them in her book *The Popular Scottish Terrier*, first published in 1955. For the most part, the descriptions of the dogs given here will have been taken from her writings.

This book will not detail the specific dogs of each decade who made a mark upon the breed, but rather certain animals will be highlighted.

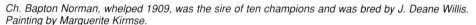

Ch. Bapton Norman, whelped 1909, was the sire of ten champions and was bred by J. Deane Willis. Painting by Marguerite Kirmse.

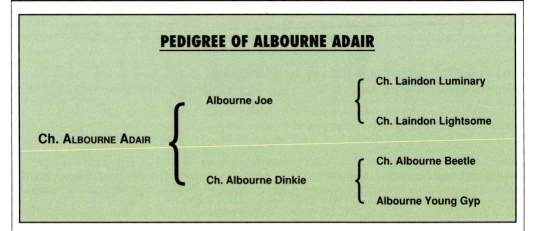

PEDIGREE OF ALBOURNE ADAIR

Ch. ALBOURNE ADAIR
- Albourne Joe
  - Ch. Laindon Luminary
  - Ch. Laindon Lightsome
- Ch. Albourne Dinkie
  - Ch. Albourne Beetle
  - Albourne Young Gyp

These dogs, because of their genetic makeup, made a major contribution to the breed.

In 1909, Mr. J. Deane Willis bred a dog named Bapton Norman, and this dog brought elements into the breed that had not been seen before. He was described as being shorter in back and straighter in front than most of the breed, and he presented a very well-balanced picture. He became a champion at two years of age, and this was considered to be quite an accomplishment for the day. He had a neat but somewhat blocky head and a dominating personality. His ears were said to be set too far forward and were slightly rounded at the tips. In addition, his body was placed more on top of his legs rather than being slung between them. Perhaps because of his smartness and style, and disregarding some faults that were discussed and criticized at great length, he was used extensively at stud. Having been used so widely, he left both good and bad qualities as his inheritance. Ch. Bapton Norman sired ten American champions.

Bapton Norman had a brother by the name of Bapton Noble. Noble was not as successful in the show ring and consequently was used less frequently at stud. However it was through Noble that this line was perpetuated when, three generations later, a dog by the name of Laindon Luminary was whelped. Luminary proved to be another pillar of the breed.

Luminary was born in 1915 and became a champion in 1920. He was used extensively at stud and this was the dog who became the link between the earlier dogs and the so-called modern Scottish Terrier. Luminary was long-headed, heavily built and low to the ground. He sired seven British champions.

Albourne Adair, a grandson of Ch. Laindon Luminary, was whelped in 1920. Mrs. Caspersz described this dog as "one of the forerunners of an improved type as regards a pleasing combination of substance with quality."

In 1925 another star came upon the scene with the whelping of

Albourne Barty. The key dog in this pedigree was Ch. Laindon Luminary and Albourne Barty became the link from Laindon Luminary to the future. He was the sire of nine champions. Mrs. Caspersz wrote: "Ch. Albourne Barty excelled in body, bone, substance and quarters... he proved quite the dog of the moment both on the bench and at stud. He was very short, thick, low to the ground and weighed about 20 pounds. His head was considered thick and his muzzle short, however, he was a balanced dog."

In 1927 an outstanding young male, a great-grandson of Ch. Albourne Adair, appeared and after passing through several hands eventually found his home with Robert Chapman and the Heather Kennels. Named Heather Fashion Hint, this was again a new type of Scottie and a dog that revolutionized the breed. He was the winner of 20 challenge certificates and the sire of 16 champions. His description,

again by Mrs. Caspersz, follows here in its entirety since this Scot made such a profound impact upon the breed.

"His critics maintained that such exaggerated length of head allied to such a short, thick body verged upon the grotesque. His tail was absurdly out of proportion, a wee rudder like an inverted carrot and carried always stiffly erect, even when the dog was sitting. He had a head of excessive length for those days, but of good shape, adorned by neat little ears well placed, and small dark eyes set well under the brow . . . His chest was the right breadth, with his body well slung between his straight, heavily boned forelegs."

Ch. Heather Necessity sired Heather Fashion Hint in 1929 and Heather Ambition in 1931. Ch. Heather Ambition's pedigree follows so that readers can see the close linebreeding with which these breeders bred their dogs. Mrs. Caspersz said, "It can be seen that intelligent

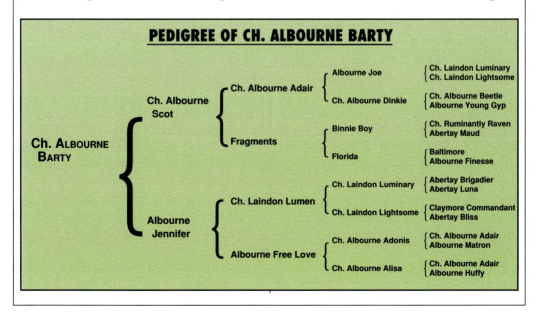

PEDIGREE OF CH. ALBOURNE BARTY

Ch. ALBOURNE BARTY
- Ch. Albourne Scot
  - Ch. Albourne Adair
    - Albourne Joe
      - Ch. Laindon Luminary
      - Ch. Laindon Lightsome
    - Ch. Albourne Dinkie
      - Ch. Albourne Beetle
      - Albourne Young Gyp
  - Fragments
    - Binnie Boy
      - Ch. Ruminantly Raven
      - Abertay Maud
    - Florida
      - Baltimore
      - Albourne Finesse
- Albourne Jennifer
  - Ch. Laindon Lumen
    - Ch. Laindon Luminary
      - Abertay Brigadier
      - Abertay Luna
    - Ch. Laindon Lightsome
      - Claymore Commandant
      - Abertay Bliss
  - Albourne Free Love
    - Ch. Albourne Adonis
      - Ch. Albourne Adair
      - Albourne Matron
    - Ch. Albourne Alisa
      - Ch. Albourne Adair
      - Albourne Huffy

PEDIGREE OF ENG. CH. HEATHER AMBITION*

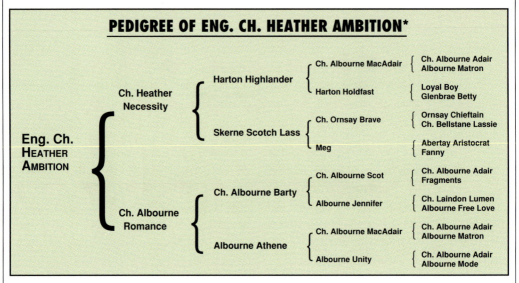

Eng. Ch. HEATHER AMBITION			
Ch. Heather Necessity	Harton Highlander	Ch. Albourne MacAdair	Ch. Albourne Adair / Albourne Matron
		Harton Holdfast	Loyal Boy / Glenbrae Betty
	Skerne Scotch Lass	Ch. Ornsay Brave	Ornsay Chieftain / Ch. Bellstane Lassie
		Meg	Abertay Aristocrat / Fanny
Ch. Albourne Romance	Ch. Albourne Barty	Ch. Albourne Scot	Ch. Albourne Adair / Fragments
		Albourne Jennifer	Ch. Laindon Lumen / Albourne Free Love
	Albourne Athene	Ch. Albourne MacAdair	Ch. Albourne Adair / Albourne Matron
		Albourne Unity	Ch. Albourne Adair / Albourne Mode

*All "Ch." designations have been earned from the Kennel Club (England).

line-breeding will do much for setting a consistent type that a breeder is looking for." Advice that is as sage today as it was 75 years ago.

Ch. Heather Ambition was the grandsire of Heather Asset, imported to America by Deephaven Kennels, where he sired 16 champions and was the great grandsire of Ch. Carnation Golden Girl, first wheaten to win a best in show.

Fashion Hint sired 13 English champions and 26 American champions without ever leaving England. Fashion Hint sired Ch. Heather Realization, who for 50 years held the record number of challenge certificates won in England. He was described as a "pocket Hercules" and unfortunately died at the age of three, having won 43 challenge certificates and 22 best in shows.

Fayette Ewing, well-known American Scottish Terrier breeder, made several trips to England prior to the 1940s and wrote of the various English champions in his book, *The Book of the Scottish Terrier*. Mr. Ewing named the prepotent English dogs of this era as Ch. Heather Necessity, Ch. Albourne Barty, Marksman of Docken and his litter sister, Albourne Annie Laurie. Dr. Ewing called them "The Four Horsemen" and wrote that these four dogs revolutionized the breed.

Barty and Necessity have been described previously but it would be remiss to complete this chapter without a mention of Marksman of Docken and Albourne Annie Laurie.

Albourne Annie Laurie, a hard-coated red brindle whelped in 1924, was bred to Ch. Albourne Barty and produced the greatest litter to be bred up to that time. The litter contained three English champions plus two other litter mates who both won challenge certificates. Annie Laurie was described as a full-sized bitch

Advertisement for Ch. Heather Realisation and kennelmates. Realisation was the winner of 11 challenge certificates and six prestigious cups from both English and Scottish best in show wins.

Albourne Annie Laurie, whelped 1924.

with a slightly long body, which Dr. Ewing called a "brood bitch type." T. Allen Kirk described Annie Laurie as a one-in-a-million-type bitch that all breeders dream about. Dr. Kirk wrote, "Annie Laurie was a good bitch, closely linebred, prepotent to reproduce her good points. Bred to any stud she will produce good puppies. Linebreed her to a great stud whose faults are not doubled with hers, and not only will she produce excellent puppies but they in turn will produce good ones. Every breeder's dream!"

Annie Laurie produced six English champions, an unequalled record for the time. She was somewhat bashful, did not perform well in the ring and changed owners several times in her lifetime.

Marksman of Docken, Annie Laurie's litter mate, probably was the least of the Four Horsemen, but his description given by Mrs. Caspersz bears repeating, if for nothing more than the wonderful word picture she paints! "He was pale silver-grey in colour, a great dog in every sense of the word, grandly proportioned throughout; maybe a trifle long-cast but with great depth of brisket, ribs carried well back, strong loin, huge bone and powerful quarters. His coat texture was not his fortune, but his greatest handicap was his size, for he was built on a very large scale. He had terrific character and a perfect temperament."

With the start of World War II, dog breeding reached a standstill in the British Isles. A few diehards kept several bitches and few dog events were held in the country. 1946 saw the return of dog shows to England with the first postwar title holder being made up. In 1947, 12 Scottish Terriers received their titles and the breed was once again in good shape.

By now, American breeders had been moving ahead full force and were breeding dogs on a par with the British imports. Many British dogs were still to be imported to America, and some of these imports made a tremendous impact upon the breed.

Early Beginnings in America:

1890 to 1920

Terriers were slow to take hold in popularity in America in comparison to the sporting breeds. The terrier development coincided with the advent of dog shows, and the Scottish Terrier development followed this path. The first dog show to take place in America was in 1874, 15 years after the first dog show in England, and the first Scottish Terrier to be exhibited in America was in 1883.

Mr. John Naylor of Mt. Forest, Illinois was the first to introduce and exhibit the Scot in America. He imported the Scottish Terriers Tam Glen and Bonnie Belle, and these two dogs made their appearance at the Pittsburgh show in 1883 entered in the Rough-Haired Terrier class. Mr. Naylor continued to show his dogs through the years of 1883, 1884, and 1885, primarily making up his own competition at each show. By the late 1880s Mr. Naylor became discouraged with the struggle for breed recognition and retired from the show ring.

In the early 1890s, gentlemen Henry Brooks, Oliver Ames and J. L. Little took up the flag and continued to press for acceptance of the Scottish Terrier. Brooks and Ames formed the Wankee Kennels and made a large monetary output to import a number of good British dogs. One of these dogs became the first American Scottish Terrier champion, Ch. Tiree, son of English Ch. Alister.

Tiree was thought by many to be the best-looking Scottish Terrier in America to that time. He weighed 20 pounds, was coal black in color, had wonderful shoulders and legs, and possessed a terrier character. It was thought that he could have had a more refined head. He was Best in Show at the Philadelphia show and for a time was the top dog in the country. Miss Fannie Brooks wrote that "he had a nasty temper and fought the other dogs without warning."

In 1895 Westminster had an entry of 55 Scotties, which set a new record for the breed. This exhibit, with 39 on the benches, attracted a great deal of attention from both exhibitors and the press.

Mr. Brooks and Mr. Ames spent their money liberally to continue to import top specimens and to breed good American dogs, but after several years became discouraged at the continued lack of interest in the breed and retired from actively promoting the Scottish Terrier. Mr. Little continued to breed and import dogs but cut his expenses by not showing in the ring, thus doing little to promote the breed among the public. The breed was once again on rocky ground in America and by 1898 only nine Scots were entered at Westminster.

By the late 1890s, Dr. Fayette C. Ewing from Louisiana became active in the breed, and remained active until his death 50 years later.

Tiree became the first American champion in 1898.

Dr. Ewing became the leader in revitalizing the Scottish Terrier and eventually was called the "Dean of Scottish Terriers." Again, this was not an easy battle for Dr. Ewing as he had not only the job of promoting and publicizing the breed but the difficulty of working against the Eastern dog establishment, which did not take kindly to newcomers from the "West." Dr. Ewing wrote, "When I took up the breed, enthusiastically determined to promote it with pocket, pen, and precept, I was regarded as an interloper, as without authority as one trying to supersede others . . ." Dr. Ewing finished two of the three Scottish Terrier champions in 1900.

James Watson, in his book *The Dog Book*, wrote about the Scottish Terrier: "The Scottish Terrier's career in this country has not been a bed of roses. It was taken up with a vim by Mr. Brooks and Mr. Ames of Boston, and one or two others. . . but there was no popularity and we can recall the time when Mr. Brooks could not even give some of his young stock away. After that the ebb tide ran out so far that it looked as if it would never turn to flood again but along came a Westerner with a reserve stock of enthusiasm and back came the Scottie with a rush that carried it to a well-earned high-water mark. A club was established and the breed put on a substantial foundation, thanks to the energy of Dr. C. Fayette Ewing."

Mr. Watson also wrote: "Enough has been said to show that the Scottish Terrier has made his way by his own merits to a warm corner in the hearts of his admirers, and that he is gradually growing in the estimation of the public and this not on account of any special attractiveness, but his smartness and cleverness as a companion and house dog."

It should be noted that the Scottish Terrier, as true with most other purebred dog breeds in America, was championed by the well-to-do who appreciated a beautiful, well-bred dog as much as they appreciated well-bred, winning horses. It is because of this monied class that the best British dogs were able to be brought to the United States. These were the years of kennels on large estates, where possibly 100 dogs of perhaps several breeds were housed, bred, conditioned and shown. Eventually, kennel managers and handlers were brought over from the British Isles to run the kennel operations. These great kennels often remained active for two or three decades. Mr. Ewing wrote: "Wealthy sportsmen are going deep into their pockets to import many of the best specimens in the Old Country and competition in New York shows is as hot as those of London or Edinburgh."

With the advent of World War II, following the 1930s Depression, dog breeding and exhibiting changed and it was no longer the sport and preserve of only the wealthy. At the present time, a kennel housing ten to 20 dogs is considered a large kennel. In addition, the owner is raising the litters, cleaning the pens, and often showing and conditioning the dogs. With luck, present-day kennels are able to find a reliable high school student to come in the afternoons and help out. Breeding and showing is now a labor of love.

In 1906 Walescott Kennel was established in New Jersey by Francis G. Lloyd. Again, many dogs were imported from Britain and became winners on the American shores. Walescott Kennels would bring from ten to 25 entries to Westminster. Mr. Lloyd died unexpectedly in 1920 and his kennel was disbanded. He was a past

Ch. Tickle 'Em Jock was the first Scot to win the prestigious Westminster Kennel Club show in 1911.

president of the Scottish Terrier Club of America and a perpetual memorial was donated to the club in his name, and is still awarded yearly to the Scottish Terrier with the greatest number of best of breed wins for the year.

In 1911 a three-and-one-half-year old Scott Ch. Tickle 'em Jock went Best in Show at Westminster over an entry of 3200 dogs. This win did much to popularize the breed among the public. English-bred and imported by Andrew Albright, Jr., Jock sired three champions but had little influence on the breed.

1910 through 1920 saw the importation of many British dogs and bitches. In 1913 two bitches were brought over from the Bapton Kennels: English Ch. Bapton Beryl and English Ch. Ems Troubadour, both sired by English Ch. Bapton Norman. Troubadour was defeated only once in the show ring on either side of the Atlantic. Beryl was thought to be the closest to the standard of any dog to that time, but she died while whelping her first litter; thus she had little impact upon the breed.

Dr. Ewing imported numerous English champions as well as breeding many of his own under the kennel prefix of Nosegay. He wrote the first extensive book on the breed in 1931, and also wrote a monthly column in one of the leading canine magazines of the time. The Nosegay prefix was well known at the dog shows.

Dr. Ewing continued to bring over a number of top British dogs, which strengthened his kennel extensively. Nosegay Sweet William was the first American-bred Scottish Terrier to take Winner's Dog at Westminster, under the largest entry of Scots up to that time. Dr. Ewing wrote that Sweet William was run over by a train shortly after that win . . .

Dr. Ewing continued his campaign for the breed, both in the show ring and through his writings in various sporting journals of the time. By the late 1910s, the breed was well established and on its way to becoming not only a beloved pet of the general population but a formidable competitor in the show ring.

Ch. Jeannie Deans, whelped 1919, bred by C. Young and owned by John MacOwen, was a group winner at Westminster in 1922.

Major Developments— Breeders and Dogs:
1920 to 1940

The period from 1920 to 1940 saw startling progress in the popularity of the Scottish Terrier. Top-producing and top-winning dogs were imported from Britain and were making a major impact upon the breed. In addition to the importation of dogs, handlers and kennel managers also crossed the Atlantic, bringing their extensive skills and knowledge to America. Bill Prentice, Scotsman from Barlae Kennel, showed and advised the Stalters of Barberry Knowe Kennels; his son Phil and daughter Florence continued on when Bill retired from the dog scene; Percy Roberts, an English man who became a highly regarded all-breed judge in America, brought over top English dogs for American breeders who were looking for outstanding stock; later, Johnny Murphy, soccer player from Scotland, became a well-known dog man throughout the country. Through the efforts of these and other gentlemen from the British Isles, the breed made dramatic improvements in America throughout the 1920s and 1930s.

The kennels, their owners and the imported dogs were numerous during this period. Scottish Terrier fanciers who are currently breeding, and have been active in the breed for two or three decades, will remember the dogs from these years, and some will have seen them in the ring. And for all of the "old-time" breeders, many of the dogs that will be mentioned here can be found in the pedigrees of their first dogs. For those starting on the road to becoming a breeder in the 1990s, they will find these dogs in their pedigrees too, although it would take effort and considerable time to trace a pedigree back through enough generations.

Ch. Albourne Adair, the key dog on the Necessity and Barty lines, was imported to America around 1922. Adair eventually went to the Ardmore Kennels in Detroit, where owner Robert McKinven used him extensively at stud. Bob McKinven retired in 1937 after breeding 15 or so champions. Adair was described by Dr. Kirk as a "nicely built black dog weighing 20 pounds, short of back with good hindquarters and tail set. He was rather plain in head, and his whiskers were rather spiky. It is interesting to note that he had a ring around his tail, a characteristic passed on to his progeny for generations." Adair was at the head of a long line of American winners, and Robert McKinven's name has gone down in the breed as one of the greats of the twenties and thirties.

John MacOwen of Mine Brook owned Ch. Jeannie Deans, considered to be a great bitch in the early 1920s. She was low set and cobby and described as having everything one would want in a Scottish Terrier.

Mr. and Mrs. E. F. Maloney owned and operated the great Goldfinder Kennels for many years. The list of good dogs owned and bred by this kennel was long, even though it was considered to be a fairly small kennel. The Maloneys owned the well-known Ch. Heather Goldfinder, sire of nearly 20 champions. Their most successful show dog was Ch. Goldfinder's Admiral, showed during the early 1950s. Mr. Maloney's interest in the breed extended over several decades until his death.

During this period the breed was further popularized by several public figures who were often in the news. Foremost in this category was U.S. President Franklin D. Roosevelt, and his Scottie Fala. Fala was often pictured with the President and was a great favorite with the press. Living to two days short of his 12th birthday, Fala was buried in the rose garden at Hyde Park, six feet away from his beloved master. In my box of "Things to Save" I have a letter dated January 9, 1944 from my aunt who was working in Washington, D.C.: "I want to tell you about 'Fala,' the President's black Scottie dog. You have probably seen

Ch. Heather Goldfinder, whelped 1929, bred by J. Cathcart and was the sire of 19 champions.

Fala, the famed Scot of President Franklin D. Roosevelt, enjoying a drive over the Hyde Park Estate.

his pictures and read about him. Well, in the office where we work, we can look out the window and see the President's backyard and we have seen 'Fala' out in the yard running around. He has a nice little green bench that he can sit on when he is tired from running around the yard. We have not seen the President yet, but if we do I shall write you and tell you so." The fancy itself was displeased with the President as he refused to trim Fala in the Scottie manner, liking the rough-and-tumble look of an untrimmed Scottie.

S. S. Van Dyne of Sporran Kennels, which once housed over one hundred Scotties, was the well-known mystery writer who wrote

Scottie bookends from 1930s.

Bronze Scottish Terrier with mouse by Marguerite Kirmse from the author's collection.

Scottie doorstops from 1920s.

The Kennel Murder Case, with a Scottish Terrier as one of the primary characters. Marguerite Kirmse of Tobermory Kennels, a well-known terrier artist, did particularly charming etchings and bronzes of the breed, which were great favorites of the public. These pieces have become highly prized, hard to find, and costly to buy.

It was during the 1930s that the Scottish Terrier reached the height of its popularity. The breed placed third in American Kennel Club registrations during the years 1933, 1936, 1937 and 1938. In 1936, 8,359 Scots were registered for the year. With the popularity of the breed, and with the number of exceptional dogs doing extensive winning, this was indeed the "Golden Era of the Scottish Terrier."

To continue on with noteworthy dogs and kennels of the 1930s: Marie Stone of Kinclaven Kennels in Milwaukee was well known and highly regarded. Mrs. Stone's kennel started in the late twenties and over 35 champions were produced and shown

Ch. Kinclaven Wild Oats, bred and owned by Marie Stone of Kinclaven Kennels.

by her until her death several decades later. She bred some of the best wheatens that the country had seen to that time. Of note was Ch. Kinclaven Wild Oats, who was described as being an excellent wheaten with great color, clean skull and the correct eye.

Relgalf Kennel, owned by Mrs. Mark Mathews, was another kennel of the '30s that was active in breeding and importing dogs. Ch. Flornell Soundfella, son of Heather Necessity, was imported in 1936, and won two best in shows and a Group Second at Westminster in 1937. In an advertisement in *The American Kennel Club Blue Book of Dogs, 1938*, it was noted that the kennel had nine bitches to be bred during 1938 and nine champion males available at stud. The kennel closed in 1948.

In the Midwest, a very successful kennel was established in Minneapolis by T. W. Bennett. Named Deephaven, for the area in which it was located, the kennel started up in the early 1930s. Bob Bartos was the kennel manager from the beginning until the kennel closed in 1947, at which time Bob left Deephaven to become kennel manager for Carnation Kennels in Washington. Over 20 champions were bred at Deephaven and top imports were brought over from England. English Ch. Crich Certainty, son of Heather Necessity, sired ten champions. This kennel made a major impact upon the breed in the 1940s through several dominant stud dogs.

Another kennel started in the late '30s that made an impact upon the breed was the Edgerstoune Kennels of Mrs. John G. Winant, wife of the U.S. wartime ambassador to England. At one time this was the largest and most successful kennel in the country. Among the imports of the 1930s were: Ch. Heather Benefactress of Edgerstoune and Ch. Ortley Ambassador of Edgerstoune.

The kennel foundation was laid in the 1930s, and the 1940s saw some great homebreds, particularly Ch. Edgerstoune Troubadour, sire of 35 champions and top stud dog for the breed up to that time. The kennel owned or bred over 100 champions.

Marlu Kennels, owned by Mr. and Mrs. Maurice Pollak, was also started during the 1930s and achieved considerable success in the mid-1930s and 1940s.

As can be seen by this overview of the dogs and kennels that made an impact on the breed in this period, the English imports were at the top of the list. Between 1930 and 1935, 54% of all finished Scottish Terrier champions were imports. 80% of the champions were sired by British dogs and only 18% had American sires and dams. The Americans were building a firm foundation for the breed and by the mid-1940s, the statistics were changing drastically.

"Lady" as "Fala" with Ralph Bellamy as F.D.R. in Sunrise at Campobello. Courtesy of Bertha Russell, Lady's owner.

The Breed Progresses:
1940 to 1965

With the advent of the Second World War, the sport of dogs continued to exist but on a much more limited scale. The STCA continued to hold their national specialities and Scots continued to earn their championships during this period. It was noted that of the 100 or so dogs completing their championships during the war years, 79 were bred before the war started.

In England, the situation became much more difficult during these years. Many kennels closed, breeding was at an absolute minimum and a number of good dogs were sent out of the country. With rations severely limited, those who did keep dogs had to share their meager supplies with their animals. Betty Penn-Bull noted in her book that this had at least one positive effect on the breed in as much as it culled the poor stock and only the better dogs were retained. The litters bred were carefully thought out and few inferior litters were whelped. Shows were very limited and transportation was difficult. In spite of the extreme difficulties in the British Isles, breeders were able to maintain enough of their breeding stock to again produce top specimens after the war, and these were dogs who made a significant impact on both sides of the Atlantic.

Winners of the American national specialties during the years of 1936 through 1947 came from the Relgalf Kennels, with the exceptions of the years of 1944 and 1947. This kennel closed in 1948 and the Relgalf name disappeared from pedigrees in fairly short order. Ch. Relgalf Rebel Leader was their best known dog, having won the Lloyd Memorial trophy for the years 1945 through 1948, and having sired ten champions.

Marlu Kennel, established in the early thirties by Maurice Pollak, imported several good dogs, including English Ch. Walsing Warrant, in addition to having bred a number of top winners. Ch. Marlu Milady was the Lloyd winner for 1937. Ch. Marlu Crusader was the sire of the brothers Ch. Deephaven Red Seal and Ch. Deephaven Jeffrey. Ch. Deephaven Warspite and Red Seal both eventually went to the Marlu Farm where the dogs were shown by Johnny Murphy. Later, Red Seal was sold to Carnation Farm.

Deephaven Kennel existed from the early 1930s until 1950. Twenty-four champions came out of Deephaven, many who in turn produced top-winning Scots. Four champion bitches produced a total of 16 champions. Three of the great Deephaven males produced a total of 38 champions. Ch. Deephaven Warspite, whelped in 1941 and the son of Ch. Hillcote Laddie, who was himself the sire of 15 champions,

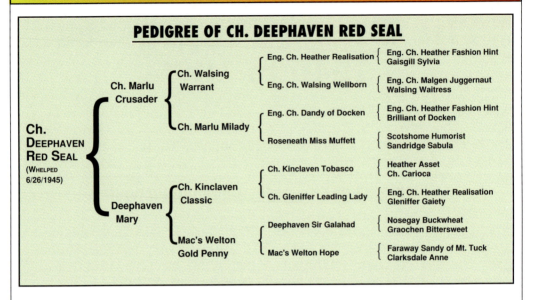

PEDIGREE OF CH. DEEPHAVEN RED SEAL

Ch. Deephaven Red Seal (Whelped 6/26/1945)

- **Ch. Marlu Crusader**
  - **Ch. Walsing Warrant**
    - Eng. Ch. Heather Realisation
      - Eng. Ch. Heather Fashion Hint
      - Gaisgill Sylvia
    - Eng. Ch. Walsing Wellborn
      - Eng. Ch. Malgen Juggernaut
      - Walsing Waitress
  - **Ch. Marlu Milady**
    - Eng. Ch. Dandy of Docken
      - Eng. Ch. Heather Fashion Hint
      - Brilliant of Docken
    - Roseneath Miss Muffett
      - Scotshome Humorist
      - Sandridge Sabula
- **Deephaven Mary**
  - **Ch. Kinclaven Classic**
    - Ch. Kinclaven Tobasco
      - Heather Asset
      - Ch. Carioca
    - Ch. Gleniffer Leading Lady
      - Eng. Ch. Heather Realisation
      - Gleniffer Gaiety
  - **Mac's Welton Gold Penny**
    - Deephaven Sir Galahad
      - Nosegay Buckwheat
      - Graochen Bittersweet
    - Mac's Welton Hope
      - Faraway Sandy of Mt. Tuck
      - Clarksdale Anne

had an impressive show record (best in show at his first outing), in addition to siring seven champions.

Ch. Deephaven Jeffrey sired six champions. Of course, the greatest dog from this kennel was Ch. Deephaven Red Seal, sire of 25 champions, including Ch. Goldfinder's Admiral, who himself was the sire of 14 champions. Red Seal is still considered a great cornerstone of the breed. Some years ago, John Sheehan of Firebrand Kennel took me by the old Deephaven Kennel building. All that remained of the kennel were the Scottie cutouts on the shutters. Now, the area has been incorporated into a beautiful suburb of Minneapolis and the kennel building is long gone.

Edgerstoune Kennels functioned from the 1920s until its closing in 1954. In the 1930s

Ch. Walsing Winning Trick of Edgerstoune, whelped 1946, won Westminster in 1950 and sired 23 champions, including Ch. Edgerstoune Troubadour.

two of the well-known imports were Ch. Ortley Ambassador of Edgerstoune, sire of 11 champions, and Ch. Walsing Winning Trick, sire of 23 champions. Trick, a black dog with consummate showmanship, was Best in Show at Westminster in 1950. He won a total of 28 bests,

The Laird of Scots Guard, sire of 13 champions, and Ch. Trojan Elm Hall, sire of 11 champions. The Carters of the Rebel Run Kennel in Louisville had two other big winners sired by Troubadour: Ch. Rebel Invader, winner of the Lloyd trophy in 1954, and Ch. Rebel Raider, sire of

PEDIGREE OF CH. EDGERSTOUNE TROUBADOUR

Ch. Edgerstoune Troubadour
- Ch. Walsing Winning Trick of Edgerstoune
  - Walsing War Parade
    - Ch. Malgen Juggernaut
    - Ch. Walsing Wishing
  - Walsing Whymper
    - Walsing Watchmaker
    - Walsing Wildwind
- Ch. Edgerstoune Orphan
  - Ch. Heather Commodore of Edgerstoune
    - Ch. Heather Resolution of Edgerstoune
    - Ch. Walsing Wishing
  - Edgerstoune Ophelia
    - Ch. Ortley Ambassador of Edgerstoune
    - Ch. Heather Ophelia of Edgerstoune

including the great shows of Morris and Essex, Westchester, Westbury, Eastern Dog Club and the Chicago International. He won the Lloyd trophy in 1949 and was the sire of the great Ch. Edgerstoune Troubadour.

Ch. Edgerstoune Troubadour, owned by Dr. and Mrs Stephen Carter, was Best in Show at the Chicago International in 1952 and Westchester in 1954, and had a total of 13 bests. He was the Scot of the year for 1951 and 1952. Troubadour was the sire of 35 champions, including Ch.

Ch. Gaidoune Gorgeous Hussy, dam of 12 champions.

Ch. Edgerstoune Troubadour, sired by Walsing Winning Trick of Edgerstoune ex Ch. Edgerstoune Orphan, was himself the sire of 35 champions.

Shieling Kennel, established in the 1930s, was owned by Mr. and Mrs. T. Howard Snethen. This kennel was exceptional for the times, as it produced top winners and top producers without the assistance of any professional help. Mr. Sneethen conditioned and showed his dogs and became a force to be reckoned with in the ring. Among the winning dogs from this kennel were Ch. Shieling's Stylist, Ch, Shieling's Designer, Ch. Shieling's Keynoter and Ch. Shieling's Master Key, all best in show dogs. The high point for this kennel was reached in 1945 when Ch. Shieling's Signature topped all dogs at Westminster for the Best in Show award, an extremely difficult feat for an

Ch. Shieling's Signature made Shieling Kennel proud in 1945 by winning Westminster, owned-handled by T. Howard Snethen. He sired 23 champions.

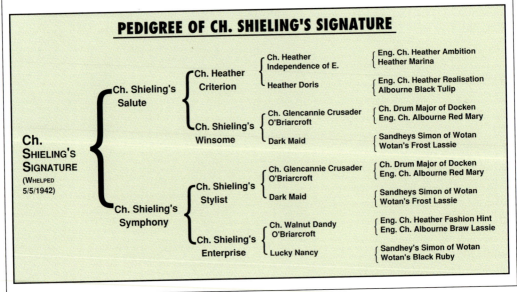

PEDIGREE OF CH. SHIELING'S SIGNATURE

Ch. SHIELING'S SIGNATURE (Whelped 5/5/1942)

- Ch. Shieling's Salute
  - Ch. Heather Criterion
    - Ch. Heather Independence of E.
      - Eng. Ch. Heather Ambition
      - Heather Marina
    - Heather Doris
      - Eng. Ch. Heather Realisation
      - Albourne Black Tulip
  - Ch. Shieling's Winsome
    - Ch. Glencannie Crusader O'Briarcroft
      - Ch. Drum Major of Docken
      - Eng. Ch. Albourne Red Mary
    - Dark Maid
      - Sandheys Simon of Wotan
      - Wotan's Frost Lassie
- Ch. Shieling's Symphony
  - Ch. Shieling's Stylist
    - Ch. Glencannie Crusader O'Briarcroft
      - Ch. Drum Major of Docken
      - Eng. Ch. Albourne Red Mary
    - Dark Maid
      - Sandheys Simon of Wotan
      - Wotan's Frost Lassie
  - Ch. Shieling's Enterprise
    - Ch. Walnut Dandy O'Briarcroft
      - Eng. Ch. Heather Fashion Hint
      - Eng. Ch. Albourne Braw Lassie
    - Lucky Nancy
      - Sandhey's Simon of Wotan
      - Wotan's Black Ruby

owner-handler. Signature, sire of 23 champions, was closely linebred on the Heather line.

Blanche Reeg of Blanart Kennels started in Scotties in the early 1930s but did not achieve prominence until 1947, when Blanart Barcarolle was whelped. Finished in 1949, she re-

and Ch. Blanart Barrister, produced a total of 34 champions between them.

Ch. Blanart Bewitching, grand-daughter of Barcarolle, had an impressive show record with seven bests in show, 20 group firsts and winner of the Terrier Group twice at

Ch. Blanart Bewitching, "Witchie," whelped 1957, by Blanart Bolero ex Blanart Bit of Bitters, won 13 consecutive specialty bests and 7 bests in show. She won the Group at Westminster twice and was the dam of seven champions.

tired from the show ring to the whelp-ing box, eventually producing ten champions. Her progeny has pro-duced close to 60 champions. Barcarolle was a big, black bitch with a good eye, ear and expression. Two of her sons, Ch. Blanart Bolero

Westminster, in addition to Best in Show at the Chicago International. She won the Lloyd trophy for 1959 and 1960. Bewitching was the dam of seven champions. Some 40 cham-pions came out of Mrs. Reeg's kennel. Especially noteworthy is that

Ch. Blanart Barcarolle, dam of ten champions, shown by Mrs. Reeg.

Above: Ch. Blanart Bolero, by Ch. Barberry Knowe Rascal ex Ch. Blanart Barrister, was the sire of 20 champions. **Below:** Ch. Blanart Barrister, sire of 14 champions, shown by Mrs. Reeg.

Mrs. Reeg did all of the conditioning and handling herself.

Mr. E. H. Stuart of Carnation Kennels began a lifelong interest in Scottish Terriers in the 1920s when he lived in Wisconsin and knew Marie Stone from Kinclaven Kennels. In the 1930s, Mr. Stuart moved to Washington State and the Carnation Kennel had its start. Bob Bartos, kennel manager of Deephaven Kennel, went to Carnation in 1947 as the kennel manager, whereupon the kennel began a decade or more of outstanding successes. The first homebred champion from Carnation was Ch. Carnation Classic.

When Bob arrived at the kennel, he imported Eng. Ch. Reimill Radiator, son of English Ch. Westpark Masterpiece, who was sired by Waltsing Wizard. Radiator was the sire of 22 champions and Masterpiece sired nine champions. A few years later, English Ch. Westpark Rio Grande was imported, also sired by Masterpiece. Rio Grande was the sire of 12 English champions and 21 American champions.

The next import was English Ch. Westpark Derriford Baffie, purchased after he had won 35 challenge certificates in England. This dog had 50 consecutive best of breeds at American shows and won best in show 22 times. He sired eight English champions and

Above: Eng. Ch. Westpark Rio Grande, son of Eng. Ch. Westpark Masterpiece, sired 33 champions.
Below: Eng., Am., Can. Ch. Westpark Derriford Baffle sired 28 champions and won best in show 22 times.

20 American champions. Carnation had the first best in show wheaten with Ch. Carnation Golden Girl, best in show in 1951.

In 1964, Carnation brought over English Ch. Bardene Bingo, a dog who was to become another pillar of the breed. John Marvin wrote, "We were fortunate to be present at the 1962 National Terrier show at Leicester, England, when Bingo was but an 11-month-old puppy. He cleaned the boards in the breed and went on to Best in Show over the top terriers in England. The dog was a sensation." His record in the show ring and as a producer is still a legend. He won three best in shows from the classes to finish his American championship and three bests in a row in Canada to complete his Canadian title. He was top terrier in 1966 and was Best in Show at Beverly Hills in 1965, Santa Barbara in 1966 and Westminster in 1967. He produced 48 champions, of which 11 became top producers themselves as sires of five or more champions. One-hundred and fifteen top-producing Scottish Terriers descended from this dog, a record that will stand for many years.

Another large kennel started in the 1930s and carrying over well into the 1960s was the Barberry Knowe Kennel of Mr. and Mrs. Charles Stalter. They owned and bred a number of top-winning and

Eng. Ch. Reimill Radiator, son of Eng. Ch. Westpark Masterpiece, was the sire of 22 champions.

Eng., Am., Can. Ch. Bardene Bingo, imported to the States in 1964 by Carnation, produced a legendary 48 champions.

PEDIGREE OF ENG., AM., CAN. CH. BARDENE BINGO

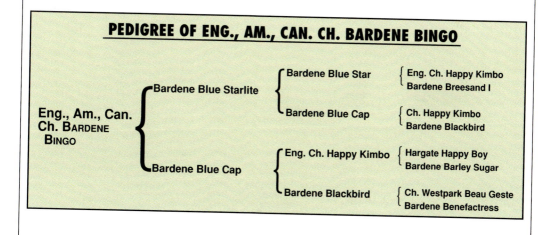

Eng., Am., Can. Ch. BARDENE BINGO	Bardene Blue Starlite	Bardene Blue Star → Eng. Ch. Happy Kimbo / Bardene Breesand I
		Bardene Blue Cap → Ch. Happy Kimbo / Bardene Blackbird
	Bardene Blue Cap	Eng. Ch. Happy Kimbo → Hargate Happy Boy / Bardene Barley Sugar
		Bardene Blackbird → Ch. Westpark Beau Geste / Bardene Benefactress

Ch. Barberry Knowe Blizzard, whelped 1952, by Ch. Walsing Wild Winter of Barberry Knowe ex Ch. Carmichael's Frivolity, was the sire of 14 champions and won best in show twice. Bred by John P. Murphy and owned by the Stalters.

The top-winning Scot for this kennel was the famous Ch. Carmichael Fanfare, bred by Ruth Johnson of Carmichael Kennel, and a top-winning bitch in the 1960s. Handled by Johnny Murphy, she won 92 bests of breed, 61 group ones and 32 bests in show. She capped her career in 1965 by becoming the fourth Scottish Terrier in the history of the breed to win the Best in Show ribbon at Westminster. "Mamie" was the dam of eight champions and she was out

top-producing Scots. Assisted originally by the Prentice family, handling was taken over in the 1960s by Johnny Murphy.

Their Ch. Barberry Knowe Barbican won the Lloyd trophy in 1951 and 1952. Top producers included Ch. Barberry Knowe Merrymaker, sire of 20 champions; Ch. Barberry Knowe Blizzard, sire of 14 champions; Ch. Barberry Knowe Wildfire, son of Blizzard and sire of 12 champions; and Ch. Barberry Knowe Revival, sire of ten champions. Ch. Barberry Knowe Conductor, son of Ch. Carmichael's Fanfare, sired 22 champions. Conductor was the sire of Ch. Dunbar's Special Agent, sire of 16 champions.

Ch. Carmichael's Fanfare won Westminster in 1965, and at the time was the greatest winning Scot in history. Bred by Ruth Johnson, shown handling, and owned by the Stalters.

Ch. Carmichael's Evening Edition, whelped 1959, by Ch. Special Edition ex Ch. Carmichael's Carmelita. Breeder-owner, Ruth Johnson.

of the kennel's top producer Merrymaker. The kennel finished nearly 90 champions.

To close out the postwar era, we will finish with Todhill Kennel, owned by Mr. and Mrs. Robert Graham. This kennel did well with both homebreds and imports. Ch. Special Edition from England was the sire of 25 champions, including the group-winning bitch Ch. Scotvale Sunshine. Other notable dogs were Ch. Todhill Cinnamon Bear, sire of nine champions, including Ch. Gaidoune Great Bear and Ch. Gaidoune Grin and Bear It. These two dogs later produced a total of 21 champions. Another in their stud force, Ch. Friendship Farm Diplomat, a grandson of Ch. Deephaven Red Seal, sired 11 champions. When Edgerstoune Kennel closed in 1954, Ch. Walsing Winning Trick of Edgerstoune moved to the Todhill Kennel. Bob Graham, although no longer breeding Scots, is still very active and vitally interested in the breed.

New kennels were springing up throughout the country as the old kennels were closing their doors. Top winners and producers were appearing on each coast. The time had arrived for easy shipment of bitches to a stud dog that lived half a continent away. Handlers and owners were flying to specialities across America and active exhibitors and breeders could take their pick of stud dogs.

Above: Ch. Carmichael's Fanfare is the dam of nine champions and won the breed 93 times, the group 61 times, best in show 32 times and seven specialtiy best of breed. *Below*: Ch. Balachan's Night Hawk, a multi-best-in-show winner, handled by breeder Evelyn Kirk winning under breeder-judge Robert Marshall.

Above: Ch. Deephaven Red Seal, owned by Carnation Farm Kennel, was the sire of 25 champions, including Ch. Goldfinder's Admiral. **Below:** Ch. Bardene Bobby Dazzler, whelped 1963, by Eng., Am., Can. Ch. Bardene Bingo ex Bardene Barefoot Contessa, was the sire of 32 champions. Breeder, Walter Palethorpe. Owners, Miriam and Anthony Stamm.

Above: A young, winning Ch. Barberry Knowe Merrymaker, whelped 1958, by Ch. Fulluvit Festive Fling ex Ch. Barberry Knowe Wyndola, was the sire of 20 champions including the great Ch. Carmichael's Fanfare. Owner-breeders, Mr. and Mrs. Charles Stalter. *Below*: Ch. Gaidoune Grin and Bear It, whelped 1962, by Ch. Todhill's Cinnamon Bear ex Ch. Gaidoune Gorgeous Hussy, won the group 35 times plus three bests in show, and sired 14 champions. Breeder-owner, Helen Gaither.

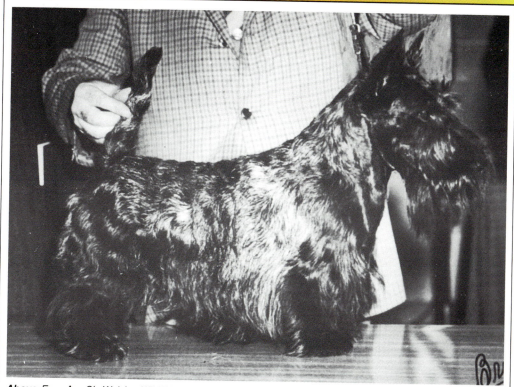

Above: Eng., Am. Ch. Walsing Wild Winter of Barberry Knowe, whelped 1958, was bred by Max Singleton and owned by Mr. and Mrs. Charles Stalter. Winner of the Lloyd trophy in 1962, he sired seven champions and was a multi-best in show winner. *Below*: Ch. Balachan Gibson Girl, whelped 1962, by Eng., Am. Ch. Viewpark Dictator ex Am., Can. Ch. Glendoone Gwenda, was the dam of nine champions. Breeder-owners, Dr. and Mrs. T. Allen Kirk, Jr.

Above: Ch. Gaidoune Gisele, whelped 1959, by Ch. Friendship Farm Diplomat ex Ch. Gaidoune Gorgeous Hussy, was the dam of 12 champions. Breeder-owner, Helen Gaither. **Below**: Ch. Gaidoune Great Bear, whelped 1960, by Ch. Todhill's Cinnamon Bear ex Ch. Gaidoune Gorgeous Hussy, was the sire of 59 champions and won 45 groups and three bests in show. Breeder-owner, H. Gaither.

Modern American Dogs:
1965 to 1990

Many new kennels were founded between the 1950s and the present time. The average life of an individual in the sport of dogs is five years and it is no different in the world of the Scottish Terrier. Families change, the show wins aren't as rapid as expected, litters are hard on a household and it all costs money. All or any of these factors can play a part on the life of an individual in dogs.

The only way to determine the quality of a kennel is to look at the records of its stock. Consistent top winners and/or top producers over a decade or two is what a top kennel is about. As history tells, great producers produce great get and they in turn produce great dogs. Kennel names that become household words are not developed overnight. It takes years of planning, work, money and dedication to build up a kennel. We cannot begin to cover all the kennels from one side of the country to the other but the kennels that are written about have met the criteria of excellence in the show ring and in the whelping box.

There were eight kennels started in the 1950s that will be mentioned in this book. Of the eight, six have closed their doors

and only two are still very actively producing and winning. These kennel names will appear in the background of nearly every well-bred Scottish Terrier today, if one takes the time to trace their pedigrees back more than a few generations.

Marlorain Kennel in Southern California began in 1952 with a partnership between Martha Melekov and Lorraine Davis. Starting with two half-sisters who were granddaughters of Ch. Deephaven Jeffrey, the kennel operated until the death of Martha in 1975. Fifty champions carried the Marlorain prefix and brought a winning tradition to the kennel.

Bob and Mildred Charves started their California kennel with two

Am, Can. Ch. Firebrand's Bookmaker, by Ch. Carnation Casino ex Ch. Firebrands's Dark Velour, is the sire of 27 champions including Ch. Sandgreg's Editorial and Ch. Sandgreg's Headline. Breeder-owner, John Sheehan.

Balachan Scots as their foundation, and by the mid-1960s they had finished nearly 30 champions. Ch. Charves Dazzler Dyke, sired by Ch. Bardene Bobby Dazzler, produced eight champions of which Ch. Charves Dashing Dawtie became the foundation bitch for the Sandgreg Kennel. This bitch, when bred to the double Bingo grandson, Ch. Firebrand Bookmaker, made a tremendous impact upon the breed. The Charves' kennel functioned until the mid-1970s.

Betty Malinka of Sandoone Kennel in Indiana started in the late 1950s and close to 30 champions came from her kennel. The top Scottish Terrier in 1975, Ch. Sandoone Royal Barclay, was the Lloyd trophy winner for the year. Sandoone Highland Heather was the dam of Ch. Dunbar's Democrat of Sandoone, sire of 48 champions. Betty remained active in the Chicago area until her death in 1978.

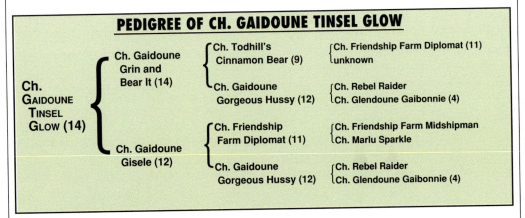

PEDIGREE OF CH. GAIDOUNE TINSEL GLOW

Ch. GAIDOUNE TINSEL GLOW (14)

- Ch. Gaidoune Grin and Bear It (14)
  - Ch. Todhill's Cinnamon Bear (9)
    - Ch. Friendship Farm Diplomat (11)
    - unknown
  - Ch. Gaidoune Gorgeous Hussy (12)
    - Ch. Rebel Raider
    - Ch. Glendoune Gaibonnie (4)
- Ch. Gaidoune Gisele (12)
  - Ch. Friendship Farm Diplomat (11)
    - Ch. Friendship Farm Midshipman
    - Ch. Marlu Sparkle
  - Ch. Gaidoune Gorgeous Hussy (12)
    - Ch. Rebel Raider
    - Ch. Glendoune Gaibonnie (4)

Ch. Gaidoune Tinsel Glow, whelped 1963, by Ch. Gaidoune Grin and Bear It ex Ch. Gaidoune Gisele, is the dam of 14 champions. Breeder-owner, Helen Gaither.

Helen Gaither's Gaidoune Kennels in West Virginia has been called the last of the great breeding kennels, and the champions and winners that came out of this kennel were extensive. Started in the late 1950s, over 100 homebred champions came from this kennel in approximately 15 years. Top sires were Ch. Gaidoune Great Bear, sire of 59 champions; and Ch. Gaidoune Grin and Bear It, sire of 14 champions. Their top-producing bitch was Ch. Gaidoune Tinsel Glow, sired by Grin and Bear It out of Ch. Gaidoune Gisele, dam of 12 champion offspring. Tinsel Glow's pedigree is shown here so that newcomers to breeding can see exactly what a tightly linebred pedigree looks like. The numbers in parentheses are the numbers of champion offspring.

Their last best in show Scot, Ch. Gaidoune Gearge W. Bear, represented seven generations of Gaidoune breeding. By 1976 they had 20 best in show winners, and 40 group winners in a 20-year period. Extensive help was given to the kennel by Dr. Nancy Lefensky, kennel manager and handler until the mid-70s.

Dr. T. Allen and Evelyn Kirk's Balachan Kennel from Roanoke, Virginia saw their first champion in 1957. The Balachan prefix was carried by

Ch. Gaidoune Gorgeous Hussy, whelped 1956, bred by Helen B. Gaither, by Ch. Revel Raider ex Ch. Glendoune Gaibonnie, was the dam of 12 champions.

Above: *Ch. Balachan Nighthawk, whelped 1964, by Am., Can. Ch. Balachan Agitator ex Ch. Balachan Gibson Girl, was owned-handled by breeders Dr. and Mrs. T. Allen Kirk to four bests in show and two specialty bests of breed.* **Below**: *Eng., Am. Ch. Gosmore Gillson Highland King, imported by Clive and Mabel Pillsbury and later owned by Richard Hensel of Dunbar Kennels, was the sire of 44 champions, including Ch. Dunbar's Democrat of Sandoone.*

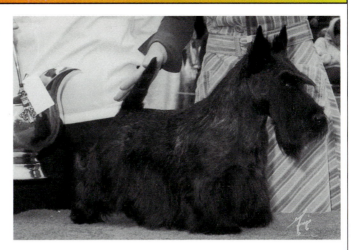

Ch. Dunbar's Democrat of Sandoone, whelped 1974, bred by Betty Malinka and owned by Richard Hensel and W.C. Crouse, was the sire of 48 champions and a multi-group and a best in show winner.

over 40 champions. Their two foundation bitches were Ch. Fran-Jean's Bridie Mollie and an English import, the breed until his death in 1992. He was a long-standing delegate to the American Kennel Club for the Scot-

PEDIGREE OF CH. DUNBAR'S DEMOCRAT OF SANDOONE

Ch. Dunbar's Democrat of Sandoone

- Eng., Am. Ch. Gosmore Gillson Highland King
  - Bardene Blue Steptoe
    - Eng., Am., Can. Ch. Bardene Bingo
    - Bardene Breesandi
  - Eng. Ch. Gillsie Highland Lass
    - Eng. Ch. Kennelgarth Viking
    - Eng. Ch. Gillsie Principal Girl
- Sandoone Highland Heather
  - Am., Mex. & Int. Ch. Reanda Rosko
    - Eng. Ch. Kennelgarth Viking
    - Eng. Ch. Kentwelle Krokus
  - Ch. Sandoone Sable II
    - Ch. Anstamm Dark Dennis
    - Sandoone Miss Jacqueline

Ch. Glendoune Gwenda. Bridie Mollie produced seven champions and her son, Ch. Balachan Agitator, sired 15 champions. Gwenda, a black-brindle, classy best in show bitch, produced six champions. Ch. Balachan Night Hawk was a owner-handled best in show winner and the winner of the Lloyd trophy in 1968.

Tom Kirk remained very active in tish Terrier Club of America, and had written a popular book on the Scottish Terrier. He was a well-known judge in the Terrier, Toy and Sporting groups. Evelyn's interest in the breed continues and she is also a respected terrier judge.

Richard Hensel of the Dunbar Kennel in Ohio started in the late 1950s and in the early 1970s acquired Ch.

Ch. Sandgreg's Headliner, by Am., Can. Ch. Firebrand's Bookmaker ex Am., Can. Ch. Charves Dashing Dawtie, was the sire of 18 champions, including the top-winning dog of all-time Ch. Braeburn's Close Encounter. Owner-handler Barbara DeSaye wins with Headliner under breeder-judge Robert Charves. Co-owner, William MacInnes.

Gosmore Gillson Highland King from the Clive Pillsburys. King became a top sire for the breed, siring 44 champions, the most famous of which was Ch. Dunbar's Democrat of Sandoone. The Democrat, bred by Betty Malinka and handled by Bergit Coady, won 18 bests-in-show, 12 specialties and 52 group firsts. The Democrat sired 48 champions, his most well-known daughter being the lovely Ch. Hughcrest Bottoms Up, producer of eight champions. He was also the sire of Ch. Democratic Victory, winner of the Lloyd trophy in 1981 and 1982. Dick was assisted with the puppy rearing by his mother, whom he fondly referred to as "the old lady."

Another popular stud in the kennel was the imported dog Ch. Reanda's King's Ransom, a grandson of Highland King. King's Ransom sired 27 champions. Altogether, the three stud dogs, Highland King, King's Ransom and the Democrat, sired a total of 119 champion get.

PEDIGREE OF AM., CAN. CH. FIREBRAND'S BOOKMAKER

Am., Can. Ch. FIREBRAND'S BOOKMAKER

- Ch. Carnation Casino
  - Am., Eng., Can. Ch. Bardene Bingo
    - Bardene Blue Starlite
    - Bardene Blue Cap
  - Ch. Carnation Cynthia
    - Ch. Westpark Derriford Baffie
    - Ch. Carnation Dark Modesta
- Am., Can. Ch. Firebrand's Dark Velour
  - Am., Eng., Can. Ch. Bardene Bingo
    - Bardene Blue Starlite
    - Bardene Blue Cap
  - Ch. Firebrand's Mustard
    - Ch. Westpark Rio Grande
    - Ch. Firebrand's Fascinator

Dick loved the world of dogs—he enjoyed breeding, judging and his dog friends. He was a very popular judge of terriers and toys, a gentleman and a true friend. The Scottish Terrier fancy was saddened by his sudden death in 1984.

John Sheehan of Firebrand Kennels in Minneapolis has had a lifelong interest in dogs, starting with a Great Dane in his childhood, moving on to Golden Retrievers in his teens and getting serious at a later date with Kerry Blue Terriers. In the mid-1950s he acquired Garthright's Dark Sorcery from Ed Jenner and finished her championship in short order. Sorcery, bred four times to Ch. Westpark Derriford Baffie, produced seven champion offspring. In her

Ch. Scotsmuir Sandpiper, by Eng., Am., Can. Ch. Bardene Bingo ex Firebrand's Dare, was the last of Bingo's sons to stand at stud. He sired 15 champions. Breeders, Bob and Jane Bartos. Owner, John Sheehan.

Ch. Anstamm Dark Venture, whelped 1962, by Eng., Am., Can. Ch. Bardene Blue Boy ex Anstamm Paragon, was the sire of 14 champions and three-time winner of the Lloyd cup.

first litter there were three group winners and two best in show dogs.

The top winner and top producer from the kennel was Ch. Firebrand's Bookmaker, double grandson of Bingo, winner of 14 bests in show, of which two were won from the classes on his first two outings. He sired 27 champions, of which one, Ch. Sandgreg's Headliner, sired 18 champions, and the other, the great Ch. Sandgreg's Editorial, sired 61 champions. Bookmaker was a short, compact, heavy-bodied dog with driving rear movement and consummate showmanship.

In the early 1970s, Bob Bartos sent Scotsmuir Sandpiper to the kennel. Sandpiper, the last Bingo son to stand at stud, finished quickly, won several groups and sired 15 champions. Sandpiper was an elegant, short black dog with the proper Scottie eye.

The kennel has consistently produced group-winning dogs and best in show winners, all conditioned and handled by John. He is still very active in breeding and in the show ring. He has been a past president of the STCA and is presently serving as delegate to the American Kennel Club.

State Senator Anthony and Miriam Stamm of Anstamm Kennels in Kalamazoo, Michigan started in the late 1950s in the breed; however, they had both been interested in Scotties prior to their marriage. In 1961 they imported English Ch. Bardene Boy Blue who finished his American championship quickly. Handled by Lena Kardos, he had a show career headed up by several bests in show and made his mark as a stud dog, siring 41 champions. He was considered to be an exaggerated type with an extra-long head, clean skull and cheeks and the correct eye—small, dark and almond shaped. He was the sire of Ch. Anstamm Dark Venture, who was the sire of 14 champions, and the first dog to sire two Lloyd trophy winners, one of which was the great Ch. Anstamm Happy Venture.

In 1965, the Stamms imported the Bingo son, Bardene Bobby Dazzler. Dazzler, more like Boy Blue than his sire, had the classic long head but was shorter in body than Boy Blue. He sired 32 champions and was the Lloyd winner for 1966.

Ch. Anstamm Dark Venture sired the dog that became another pillar of the breed, Ch. Anstamm Happy Venture. Happy Venture, out of Ch. FitzWilliam's Happy Girl, won the Lloyd trophy in 1972 and 1973 and produced a phenomenal record of 90 champions.

Included in Happy Venture's champion get was Ch. Anstamm Happy Sonata. Sonata won nine best in shows, 41 group firsts and five specialties, one of which was Montgomery County. In addition to winning the Lloyd trophy in 1978, she found time for the whelping box and produced ten champions.

Ch. Anstamm Venture On, son of Happy Venture, sired 26 champions and Ch. Anstamm Ruff-Me-Tuff Rowdy, also by Venture, sired 13 champions. Ch. Anstamm Happy Venture was the grandsire of Ch. Hughcrest Bottoms Up and Ch. Braeburn's Close Encounter, top-winning dog of all breeds of all time.

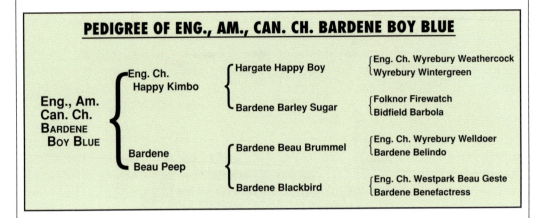

PEDIGREE OF ENG., AM., CAN. CH. BARDENE BOY BLUE

Eng., Am. Can. Ch. BARDENE BOY BLUE	Eng. Ch. Happy Kimbo	Hargate Happy Boy	Eng. Ch. Wyrebury Weathercock / Wyrebury Wintergreen
		Bardene Barley Sugar	Folknor Firewatch / Bidfield Barbola
	Bardene Beau Peep	Bardene Beau Brummel	Eng. Ch. Wyrebury Welldoer / Bardene Belindo
		Bardene Blackbird	Eng. Ch. Westpark Beau Geste / Bardene Benefactress

Eng., Am., Can. Ch. Bardene Boy Blue, whelped 1957, by Eng. Ch. Happy Kimbo ex Bardene Beau Peep, was a multi-best in show winner in three countries and the sire of 41 American champions. Owners, Miriam and Anthony Stamm.

Ch. Bardene Bobby Dazzler, whelped 1963, bred by Walter Palethorpe, was a multi-group and specialty winner and the sire of 32 champions. Owners, Anthony and Miriam Stamm.

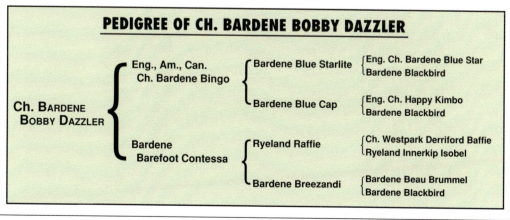

PEDIGREE OF CH. BARDENE BOBBY DAZZLER

Ch. Bardene Bobby Dazzler

- Eng., Am., Can. Ch. Bardene Bingo
  - Bardene Blue Starlite
    - Eng. Ch. Bardene Blue Star
    - Bardene Blackbird
  - Bardene Blue Cap
    - Eng. Ch. Happy Kimbo
    - Bardene Blackbird
- Bardene Barefoot Contessa
  - Ryeland Raffie
    - Ch. Westpark Derriford Baffie
    - Ryeland Innerkip Isobel
  - Bardene Breezandi
    - Bardene Beau Brummel
    - Bardene Blackbird

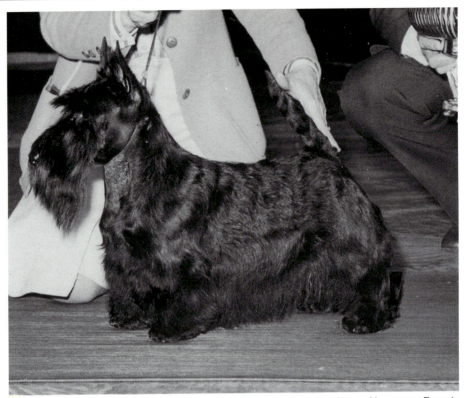

Above: Ch. Anstamm Happy Sonata, whelped 1975, by Ch. Anstamm Happy Venture ex Reanda Razziella, won nine bests in show and is the dam of ten champions. Breeders, Michael and Sharon Lowman. Owner, Miriam Stamm. *Below*: Ch. Anstamm Venture On, whelped 1979, by Ch. Anstamm Happy Venture ex Ch. Anstamm Most Likely, was the sire of 33 champions. Breeders, Miriam Stamm and Cindy Cooke.

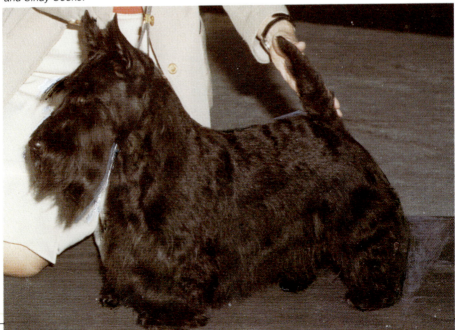

Ch. Anstamm Happy Venture, whelped 1971, by Ch. Anstamm Dark Venture ex Ch. Fitzwilliam's Happy Girl, is the all-time top-producing sire in the breed, having produced 90 champions, three of which are best in show winners. Breeders, Wilfred and Mary Schwer. Owners, Anthony and Miriam Stamm.

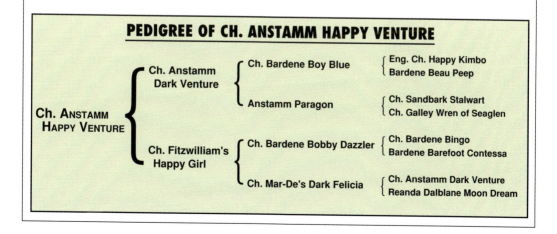

PEDIGREE OF CH. ANSTAMM HAPPY VENTURE

Ch. ANSTAMM HAPPY VENTURE

Ch. Anstamm Dark Venture
- **Ch. Bardene Boy Blue**
  - Eng. Ch. Happy Kimbo
  - Bardene Beau Peep
- **Anstamm Paragon**
  - Ch. Sandbark Stalwart
  - Ch. Galley Wren of Seaglen

Ch. Fitzwilliam's Happy Girl
- **Ch. Bardene Bobby Dazzler**
  - Ch. Bardene Bingo
  - Bardene Barefoot Contessa
- **Ch. Mar-De's Dark Felicia**
  - Ch. Anstamm Dark Venture
  - Reanda Dalblane Moon Dream

Ch. Sandgreg's Editorial, whelped 1975, by Am., Can. Ch. Firebrand's Bookmaker ex Am., Can. Ch. Charves Dashing Dawtie, was the sire of 61 champions, including Ch. Sandgreg's Second Edition. Breeder-owners, John and Barbara DeSaye.

joined the kennel. Anstamm continues to this day with impressive wins across the country. For some years the dogs have been handled and conditioned by Miriam and Cindy. The Anstamm kennel name and their influence will remain a force in the breed for many years.

As can be seen, the impact made by the three English imports, the "Three B's"—Ch. Bardene Bingo, Ch. Bardene Bobby Dazzler and Ch. Bardene Boy Blue—has been tremendous. The three produced a total of 121 champions and their top-winning descendants are countless.

John and Barbara DeSaye's Sandgreg Kennel in Michigan is the transitional kennel between the previous

Tony Stamm died in 1974 and Cindy Cooke, and later Linda Nolan, breeders and the "new guard." They acquired two bitches from the

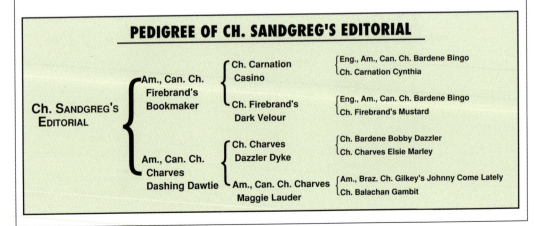

PEDIGREE OF CH. SANDGREG'S EDITORIAL

Ch. SANDGREG'S EDITORIAL

- Am., Can. Ch. Firebrand's Bookmaker
  - Ch. Carnation Casino
    - Eng., Am., Can. Ch. Bardene Bingo
    - Ch. Carnation Cynthia
  - Ch. Firebrand's Dark Velour
    - Eng., Am., Can. Ch. Bardene Bingo
    - Ch. Firebrand's Mustard
- Am., Can. Ch. Charves Dashing Dawtie
  - Ch. Charves Dazzler Dyke
    - Ch. Bardene Bobby Dazzler
    - Ch. Charves Elsie Marley
  - Am., Can. Ch. Charves Maggie Lauder
    - Am., Braz. Ch. Gilkey's Johnny Come Lately
    - Ch. Balachan Gambit

Charves and one of them, Ch. Charves Dashing Dawtie, bred to John Sheehan's Ch. Firebrand's Bookmaker, double Bingo grandson, produced two brothers who made a tremendous impact upon the breed—Ch. Sandgreg's Headliner and his younger brother, Ch. Sandgreg's Editorial.

Headliner, shown more than Editorial, sired 18 champions, including the greatest winning dog of all breeds of all time, Ch. Braeburns Close Encounter. Headliner's daughter, Ch. Braeburn's Topic of Sandgreg, produced eight champions, and a son of hers, Ch. Braeburn's Main Event, sired 25 champions. Another son, Ch. Sandgreg's Square Deal, sired 34 champions and revolutionized the wheaten Scot.

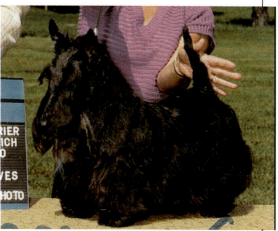

Ch. Charves Dashing Dawtie, by Ch. Charves Dazzler Dyke ex Am., Can. Ch. Charves Maggie Lauder, was the dam of seven top producers, including Ch. Sandgreg's Editorial. Breeders, Robert and Mildred Charves. Owners, John and Barbara DeSaye.

Ch. Sandgreg's Editorial, whelped in 1975, is the second leading sire in the breed with 61 champion offspring, including seven top-producing get. His son, Ch. Sandgreg's Second Edition, is the sire of 67 champions, including Ch. Brookhill's Morning Edition, top-winning Scottish Terrier and Best in Show at Montgomery County Kennel Club show in 1991 and 1992.

The Sandgregs are still very active in the breed, continuing to produce top winners and top producers. John has also been active in the STCA and is a past president of the national club.

Chris and Judy Hughes came to Scottish Terriers in the mid-1970s after a successful stint in Miniature Schnauzers. They purchased their first Scottish Terrier bitch, Sonata Seranade, an Anstamm Happy Venture daughter, and finished her championship quickly. In 1976 Ch. Sonata Seranade won two bests in show, ten group firsts and 30 group placements. She produced six champions, including Ch. Hughcrest Home Brew, sire of seven champions. Ch. Hughcrest Happy Hour, bred to Ch. Dunbar's Democrat of Sandoone, produced Ch. Hughcrest Bottoms Up, dam of five champions. Bottoms Up had a very successful show career over a seven-year period, capping it off with a Best of Breed from the Veterans class at the Montgomery County Specialty in 1985.

The Hughes remained active in the breed for about 12 years, when family commitments required a curtailing of activities. Judy only kept two dogs at a time and conditioned and showed the dogs herself, sometimes with an assist from her husband. For those who saw Judy in

Am., Can. Ch. Firebrand's Fury, by Ch. Westpark Derriford Baffie ex Ch. Firebrand's Dark Sorcery, was bred and owned by John Sheehan.

the ring, and particularly for those who competed against her, dog and handler were immaculate, smart and formidable competition.

Christine and Fred Stephens of Glenby Kennel from Oregon have made accomplishments in both the whelping box and in the show ring since the mid-1970s. Ch. Glenby Gallant Lad has sired 37 champions and is a multi-group and best-in-show specialty winner. American and Canadian Ch. Glenecker Gallivanter from England is a multi-group winner and sire of 18 champions. Ch. Glenby Royal Ruler, a Gallant Lad grandson, is a group and specialty winner and sire of 14 champions.

The Stephens family handles and conditions their own dogs and Fred is a respected terrier judge. Christine always catches the judge's eye when she enters the ring with her smartly groomed Scots.

Two more breeders who deserve mention are Debbie Brooks of Deblin Kennels in Maryland and Tom and Charla Hill of Charthill Kennels in South Carolina.

Debbie Brooks became serious about the breed in the mid-1970s. Ch. Deblin's Back Talk is a multi-group winner, winner of 15 specialties and was Best of Breed at Montgomery County in 1987 and Best of Opposite at the National in 1988. Sired by Ch. Anstamm All

Ch. Hughcrest Bottoms Up winning best of opposite sex at Montgomery County in 1981 under Betty Penn-Bull of Kennelgarth Kennels of England. Breeder Judy Hughes and presenter STCA president John Sheehan.

American, "Tony" has sired 45 champions. Approximately 30 champions presently carry the Deblin prefix. Debbie is another keen competitor in the ring, always showing a well-turned-out dog.

Tom and Charla Hill became serious in the ring in the early 1980s and their first big winner was Ch. Charthill Worthy of Colwick, a Ch. Amstamm Happy Venture grandson. "Bosworth" has sired 34 champions and is a multiple group winner and a multi-specialty winner. Ch. Charthill Tiger Rose and Ch. Charthill Seaworthy are both group winners. Approximately 40 champions have the Charthill prefix.

Time can only tell who the breeders of the future will be, who will have an impact on the breed to the extent that Deephaven Kennels, the Anstamm Kennels, Gaidoune Kennels and others have had. The breed is in good condition and through the efforts and dedication of the breeders of the future, it will remain as such.

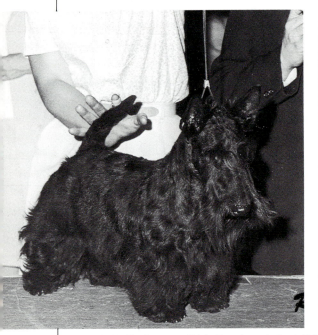

Above Left: Ch. Anstamm Bright Promise, whelped 1966, by Ch. Charves Dark Viking ex Ch. Anstamm Ebony. Breeders, Tony & Miriam Stamm. Owners, Bengt and Cynthia Wallgren. **Above Right:** Ch. Bardene Bookmark, whelped 1977, by Eng. Ch. Gaywyn Landmark ex Bardene Black Silk. Breeder, Walter Palethorpe. Owners, Bengt & Cynthia Wallgren.

Below Left: Ch. Balachan Naughty Gal, whelped 1968, by Ch. Barberry Knowe Merrymaker ex Ch. Balachan Gibson Girl. Breeders, Dr. & Mrs. T. Allen Kirk. Owner, Mrs. Charles Stalter. **Below Right:** Ch. Gren-Aery Merely A Monarch, whelped 1983, by Ch. Anstamm All American ex Ch. Gren-Aery Small Wonder. Breeder-owner, Joan Eagle.

Above Left: *Ch. Deblin's Double Talk, whelped 1986, by Ch. Sunray Summer Sun ex Ch. Deblin's Sweet Talk. Breeders, D. Brookes & L. Struck. Owners, Deborah & Anthony Brookes.* **Above Right:** *Ch. Glenby Royal Ruler. Breeders-owners, Christine & Fred Stephens.*

Below Left: *Ch. Dunbar's Democrat of Sandoone. Owners, Richard Hensel & W. Crouse.* **Below Right:** *Ch.Gren-Aery Edward, whelped 1970, by Ch. Schaeffer's Sky Rocket ex Ch. Blanart Bounce of Gren-Aery. Breeder-owner, Joan Eagle.*

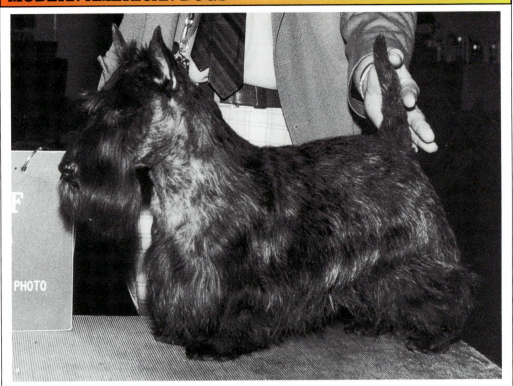

Above: *Ch. Kinsmon's Noble Heir, whelped 1974, by Ch. Sagette's Murphy's Leisure ex Sagette's Mary Dweller. Owners, Alice and Ed Watkins.*
Below: *Ch. Scarista Gloriana, whelped 1982, by Viewpark Alexander ex Millig Miss Marquessa. Owner, Sanford E. Rosenfeld.*

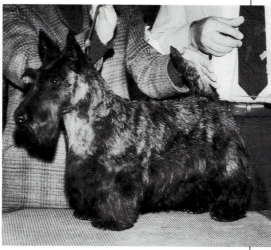

Above Left: *Ch.Ramtree Stonehedge Aleta, by Ch. Stonehedge Bandmaster ex Ch. Marlorain Lolita. Breeders, Tom Natalini, Don Massaker and Mr. & Mrs. R. Seelbach. Owners, Martha Melekov and Lorraine Davis.* **Above Right:** *Ch. Vikland's Carbon Delight. Breeder-owners, Bill & Kathy Bowers.*

Below Left: *Ch. Gren-Aery Small Wonder, whelped 1978, by Ch. Gren-Aery Edward ex Ch. Am. Anger Starlight. Breeder-owner,Joan H. Eagle.* **Below Right:** *Ch. Hughcrest Daiquiri Doll. Breeders, Judy Hughes & Roy Lay. Owners, Chris & Judy Hughes.*

Above Left: *Ch. Firebrand's Station Master, whelped 1986, by Ch. Firebrand's Ringmaster ex Firebrand's Proud Lass. Breeder-owner, John Sheehan.* **Above Right:** *Ch. Caevness Devil Due, by Ch. Charthill Worthy of Colwick ex Caevness Amy March of Alcott. Owners, Robert & Jane Phelan.*

Bottom Left: *Ch. Anstamm Shout It Out, by Ch. Anstamm Loud and Clear ex Anstamm Flash Fire's Cinder. Owners, Anstamm Kennels.* **Bottom Right:** *Ch. Democratic Victory, whelped 1978, by Ch. Dunbar's Democrat of Sandoone ex Ch. Prairyhill's Promander. Breeder, Mrs. Robert Willis. Owner, Robert Willis.*

Above Left: *Ch. Glenby's Royal Viking, by Ch. Glenby Valiant Contender ex Ch. Glenby's Lovely Lady. Breeder-owners, Christine & Fred Stephens.* **Above Right:** *Ch. Koch's Nut'n Ventur'd Nut'n Gain'd, whelped 1988, by Ch. Sandgreg's Johnny Come Lately ex Ch. Koch's Olympic Flame. Breeders, Fred & Ann Koch. Owner, Mayumi Takau.*

Below Left: *Ch. Scotsbairn's Baron Dhu. Owners, Thomas Beaman and Debby Fowler.* **Below Right:** *Ch. Perlor Perfect Match, by Gaywyn Landmark ex Penny Black of Perlor. Breeders: William & Lorrian Hall. Owners, Jack & Elizabeth Cooper.*

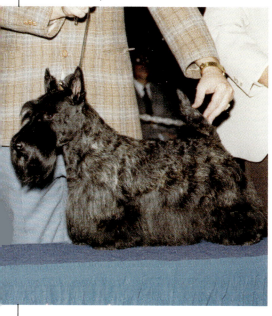

Above Left: *Ch. Kentwella Solo of Gaywyn, whelped 1987, by Eng. Ch. Stefango's Bon Voyage ex Killisport Jessica. Breeder, Mrs. Szczepanek. Owners, Tom & Sandy Lehrack.* **Above Right:** *Ch. Firebrand's Foolish Fun, by Ch. Firebrand's Goodwill ex Firebrand's Dark Abigail. Breeder, Karen Dunn. Owner, John Sheehan.*

Below Left: *Ch. Sandgreg's Foxmoor, whelped 1983, by Ch. Sandgreg's Editorial ex Am., Can. Ch. Sandgreg's Sweet Charity. Breeders, John & Barbara DeSaye. Owner, Dr. & Mrs. James Boso.* **Below Right:** *Ch. Glenby's Royal Viking, whelped 1990, by Ch. Glenby Valiant Contender ex Ch. Glenby's Lovely Touch. Breeder-owners, Christine & Fred Stephens.*

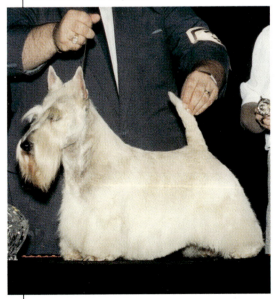

Above: Ch. Sandgreg's Second Editiion, by Ch. Sandgreg's Editorial ex Ch. Braeburn's Topic of Sandgreg. Owners, John & Barbara DeSaye.

Below: Ch. Blueberry Born to Boogie, whelped 1987, by Ch. Jabberwok Bristol Stomp ex Ch. Blueberry's Glen Glory. Breeders, Kathie Brown & Gerry Poudrier. Owner, Merle Taylor.

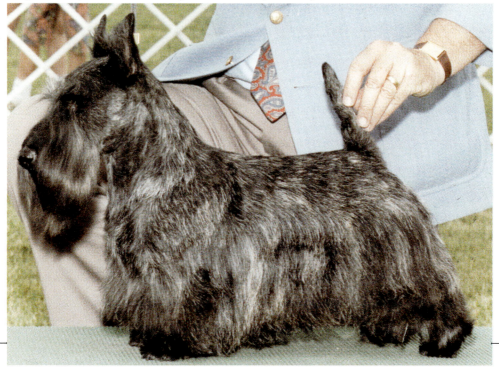

Above Left: Ch. Seaforth's Dirk The Laird, whelped 1981, by Ch. Reanda King's Ransom ex Ch. Hilcar's Royal Lady. Breeders, Seaforth's Scotties. Owners, Retha Brannan & Cathy St. John. *Above Right:* Ch. Jabberwok Bristol Stomp, whelped 1977, by Ch. Rinklestone Bryndle Bryar ex Neidfyre Bright Star. Breeders, Merle Taylor and Gail Gaines. Owners, Carolyn and Merle Taylor.

Below Left: Ch. Glengloamin's Look of Luv, by Ch. Sandgreg's Second Edition ex Ch. Sandgreg's Sweet Luv. Breeders, Dr. J. & E. Boso and B. DeSaye. Owners, Mark & Sally George. *Below Right:* Am., Can. Ch. Glenecker Gallivanter, whelped 1985, by Glenecker Brantham ex Glenecker Rye. Breeder, Mrs. Micklethwaite. Owners, Fred & Christine Stephens.

Left Above: *Ch. Am. Anger Starlight, whelped 1972, by Ch. Seagrave's Rogue's Image ex Ch. Fashion Merry Star. Breeder, Edward Jarvis. Owner, Joan H. Eagle.* **Right Above:** *Ch. Perlor Flower of Scotland, whelped 1977, by Ch. Perlor Postmark ex Ch. Perlor Principale. Breeders, William and Lorrian Hall. Owner, Elizabeth Cooper.*

Left Below: *Ch. Amescot's Lotta Talk, by Ch. Deblin's Back Talk ex Ch. That's My Girl. Owners, Harold & Carol Ames.* **Right Below:** *Ch. Seaforth's Brindi Bart, whelped 1979, by Ch. Prairyhill TopNotch ex Ch. Dunbar's Sable of Sandbark. Breeders, Seaforth's Scotties. Owner, Tanya Garza.*

Above Left: *Ch. Charthill Worthy of Colwick, whelped 1985, by Ch. Sunray Summer Sun ex Ch. Colwick Time after Time. Breeders, Tom Hill & David Luken. Owners, Tom & Charla Hill.* **Above Right:** *Ch.Ruff-Me-Tuff Roustabout, whelped 1971, by Ch. Gillsie Prince William ex Ch. Stedplane Suki. Breeder-owners, Jake & Nancy McClosky.*

Below Left: *Ch. Firebrand's Decision Maker, whelped 1985, by Ch. Hillview's Friar Tuck ex Ch. Firebrand's Hot Spice. Breeder-owner, John Sheehan.* **Below Right:** *Ch. Firebrand's Pay Mistress, by Ch. Firebrand's Paymaster ex Ch. Firebrand's Royal Pledge. Breeder-owner, John Sheehan.*

Above Left: Ch. Perlor Playboy, whelped 1978, by Int. Ch. Woodmansey Woden ex Ch. Perlor Principale. Breeders, William & Pearl Hall. Owner, Elizabeth Cooper. **Above Right:** Ch. Dana's Constant Comment, whelped 1977, by Ch. Anstamm Happy Minute Man ex Ch. Anstamm Happy Days. Breeder, Nancy Fingerhut. Owners, Ken & Betty McArthur.

Below Left: Ch. Sunrise Corsair, whelped 1983, by Ch. Anstamm Venture On ex Ch. Alohascott Sunrise Secret. Breeders-owners, Tom & Sandy Lehrack. **Below Right:** Ch. The Macgregor, by Ch. Besscott Landhire Checkmate, whelped 1989, ex Ch. Jo Dans Amber Amanda. Owned by Elizabeth Cooper and Jeannie Heyder Hunt.

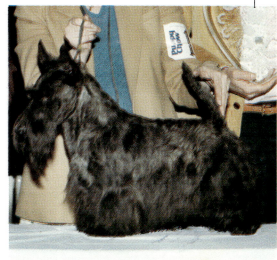

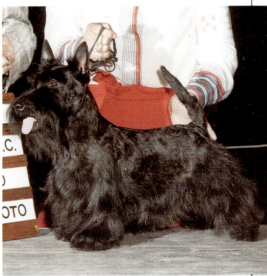

Above Left: *Am. Can. Ch. Barraglen's Beachcomber, whelped 1978, by Ch. Dunbar's Royal Heritage ex Barraglen Barmaid O'Riagain. Breeders, Ann Bower & Mary Lou Ludlow. Owner, A. Ross Bower.* **Above Right:** *Ch. Firebrand's Penny Arcade, whelped 1978, by Ch. Scotsmuir Sandpiper ex Ch. Firebrand's Pandora. Breeder-owner, Muriel Lee.*

Below Left: *Ch. Anstamm Summer Lightning, whelped 1983, by Ch. Anstamm Up Front ex Ch. Sun-Ray's Summer Day. Breeders, Linda Nolan & Cindy Cooke. Owner, Anstamm Kennels.* **Below Right:** *Ch. Hopscotch Heads We Win, by Ch. Perlor Playboy ex Ch. Hopscotch High Jinks. Owner, Mary Moran McQuinn.*

Above: Am. Can. Ch. Glenby Gallant Lad, by Eng., Am. Ch. Gaywyn Likely Lad ex Ch. Theda Theda. Owners, Fred & Christine Stephens.

Below: Ch. Sally Rand, whelped 1985, by Ch. Glenby Gallant Lad ex Ch. Scarista Gloriana. Breeder, S. E. Rosenfeld. Owners, Ken & Betty McArthur.

81

Above Left: *Int., P.R., Am. S.Am., Can. Ch. McVan's Sandman, whelped 1987, by Ch. Sandgreg's Second Edition ex Am. Can. Ch. Maggie McMuffin V. Breeder, Vandra Huber. Owners, Dr. Vandra Huber & Michael Krolewski.* **Above Right:** *Ch. Brookhill Firemist, whelped 1986, by Ch. Perlor Playboy ex Ch. MacPooch Ms Michie. Breeder, Louis Arroyo. Owners, Louis Arroyo & Betty LeClaire.*

Below Left: *Ch. Aerie Almost Heaven, whelped 1978, by Ch. Gaidoune Bicentennial Bear ex Ch. Kirk Nor Sitting Pretty. Breeder-owners, Linda Hains & H. Quarles.* **Below Right:** *Ch. Ashmoor Huck Finn of Gaelwyn, whelped 1983, by Ch. Wayridge Bold Brass O' Gaelwyn ex Gaelwyn's Touch of Class. Breeders, Lee Lawrence & Elaine Lawrence. Owner, Robert V. Moore III.*

Above Left: *Ch. Wayridge Bold Brass O'Gaelwyn, whelped 1981, by Ch. Wayridge Bold Ruler ex Ch. Wayridge Abigail. Owner, Kathy McKessor.* **Above Right:** *R-Starr Royal N'Tasha of Glenby, by Ch. Boulder Legend Landslide ex Glenby Royal Lady. Breeder-owners, Robin Starr & Chris Stephens.*

Below Left: *Ch. Anstamm Low Commotion, whelped 1989, by Ch. Anstamm Flash Point ex Anstamm Short Circuit. Breeders, Pat Pichon and Anstamm Kennels. Owners, Anstamm Kennels.* **Below Right:** *Ch. Uncanny's Starlight Express, whelped 1987, by Ch. Uncanny's Balgair's Chances R ex Ch. Uncanny's Paisley Park. Breeders, Jane & John Anderson. Owners, John & Jane Anderson and Joan Duke.*

Above Left: *Ch. Ashmoor Arts and Letters, whelped 1986, by Ch. Ashmoor Huck Finn of Gaelwyn ex Ch. Ashmoor Catcher in the Rye. Breeders, Robert Moore III & Laurie Moore. Owner, Raumond Juers.* **Above Right:** *Ch. Wychwyre Witchcraft, whelped 1986. Breeders-owners, Bill & Sue Martin.*

Below Left: *Ch. Koch's Olympic Flame, whelped 1984, by Ch. Sandgreg's Editorial ex Ch. Glad-Mac's Georgette. Breeder-owners, Fred & Ann Koch.* **Below Right:** *Am., Can. Ch. Maggie McMuffin, whelped 1984, by Ch. Sandgreg's Square Deal ex Heatherton's Ceiti Neil. Breeder, Barbar Jane Middleton. Owner, Dr. Vandra Huber.*

Above Left: Ch. Ruffton's Dynamo, by Ch. Dunbar's Democrat of Sandoone ex Ch. Dunbar's Southern Dancer. Owners, Rick & Debby Fowler. **Above Right:** Ch. Glengloamin's Luv of My Life, whelped 1988, by Ch. Sandgreg's Second Edition ex Ch. Sandgreg Sweet Luv. Owners, B. Gooch and H. Miyamura. Breeders, Dr. J. & E. Boso and B. DeSaye.
Below Left: Ch. Duff-De Fireworks, whelped 1973, by Ch. Schaeffer's Sky Rocket ex Duff-De Bonnie Bojangles. Breeder-owners, Bill & Kathy de Villeneuve. **Below Right:** Ch.Glendale's Happy Hooligan, whelped 1973, by Ch. Anstamm Happy Venture ex Glendales Misty Heather. Breeders, Ed & Jean McCormick. Owners, Robert V. Moore III.

Above Left: Ch. Braeburn's Main Event, whelped 1978, by Ch. Sandgreg's Headliner ex Ch. Anstamm Happy Moment. Breeders, Ron & Helen Girling. Owners, Bengt & Cynthia Wallgren. ***Above Right:*** Ch. Redoubt's Gaewyn's C'est Moi, whelped 1977, by Redoubt's Salute to Anstamm ex Ch. Gaelwyn's Beau's Image. Breeders, Leland and Elaine Lawrence. Owners, Donald & Carol Plott.

Below Left: Ch. Reanda King's Ransom, by Eng. Ch. Gaywyn Kingson ex Ch. Reanda Rosally. Breeder, Mrs. Elsie Meyer. Owner, Richard Hensel. ***Below Right:*** Ch. Sandgreg's Journalist, by Ch. Sandgreg's Editorial ex Ch. Sonata Serenade. Breeder-owners, John & Barbara DeSaye.

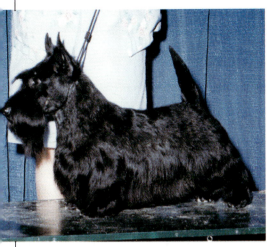

Above Left: *Am. Can. Ch. Sunrise Trick Or Treat, whelped 1989, by Ch. Kentwella Solo of Gaywyn ex Ch. J. Branigan Sentmental Dremr. Breeder, Jeffrey Schur, DVM. Owner, Tom & Sandy Lehrack, Sunrise Kennels.*
Above Right: *Am., Can. Ch. Barraglen's Bramble Heather, whelped 1987, by Ch. Whiskybae Yanky Stunt Man ex Ch. Barraglen's B Sharp. Breeders, Alan & Ann Bower. Owners, Ann Bower and Barry Truax.*

Below Left: *Ch. Redoubt's Heavenly Hash, whelped 1985, by Ch. Sandgreg's Novelist ex Ch. Snowhill Celebrate Me Lite. Breeder, Chris Davis. Owners, Carol & Donald Plott.* **Below Right:** *Ch. Besscott's Royal Flush, whelped 1984, by Ch. Perlor Playboy ex Ch. Perlor Picquant. Owners, Helen and Norman Prince.*

Ch. Ashmoor at the Ritz, whelped 1981, by Ch. Redoubt's Salute to Anstamm ex Ch. Reality Tassie Lynn. Breeder, Robert Moore III. Owners, Robert Moore III and Laurie Moore.

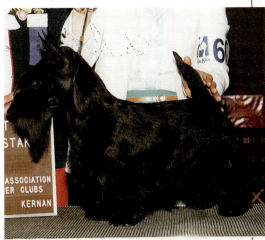

Above Left: *Eng., Ital., Am. Ch. Enchanter of Eilburn, whelped 1975, by Eng. Ch. Gillson Grandiloquence ex Maid of Merriemuir. Owner, Antonella Visconti Di Modrone.* **Above Right:** *Ch. Deblin's Small Talk, whelped 1982, by Ch. Bar-nones Dazzling Add-Venture ex Ch. Su-ets Disney Girl. Breeders, Deborah Brookes & Lynn Struck. Owners, Deborah & Anthony Brookes.*

Below Left: *Ch. Dana's Sunday Edition, whelped 1979, by Ch. Sandgreg's Editorial ex Ch. Hughcrest Hot Fudge Sunday. Breeder-owner, Nancy Fingerhut.* **Below Right:** *Ch. Glenby's Special Blend, by Ch. Glenby's Gallant Lad ex Ch. Glenby's Leading Lady. Breeder-owners, Fred & Christine Stephens.*

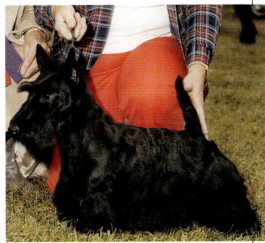

Above: Ch. Reanda Royal Sovereign, whelped 1982, by Ch. Glenecker Gulliver ex Ch. Reanda Roxanne. Breeder, Mrs. Else Meyer. Owners, Jake & Nancy McClosky.

Below: Ch. Gaywyn Nelda, whelped 1974, by Ch. Gaywyn Joel ex Ch. Gaywyn Nola. Breeder, Mrs. Muriel Owens. Owners, C. Michael & Christine E. Cook.

Above Left: *Ch. Am Anger Glendale Star, whelped 1972, by Ch. Seagrave's Rouge's Image ex Ch. Fashion Merry Star. Breeder, Edward B. Jarvis. Owners, Jean & Fred Ferries Wychwood Kennels.* **Above Right:** *Ch. Gaywyn Jazzman, whelped 1984, by Eng. Ch. Brio Wordsworth ex Ch. Macanda Baby Jane. Breeder, Muriel Owens. Owners, Tom & Sandy Lehrack, Sunrise Kennels.*

Below Left: *Ch. Dana's Gold Coin, whelped 1985, Ch. Dana's Sunday Edition ex Sterling Mill Emily. Breeder, J. Schultz. Owner, Nancy C. Fingerhut.* **Below Right:** *Am., Can. Ch. Passmore's Dona Lucha, whelped 1985, by Ch. Sandgreg's Square Deal ex Passmore's Silver Flash. Breeder, Jeannie Passmore. Owners, Jorge & Patricia Torrejon.*

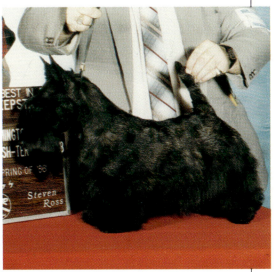

Jan Goeman participating in a fun match in Minnesota with John Sheehan.

The Scottish Terrier Club of America

The STCA, a non-profit organization, was founded in 1900 and was the 25th breed club to be recognized by the American Kennel Club.

As stated in the constitution, the purpose of the national club is:

"To encourage and promote the breeding of purebred Scottish Terriers; To encourage the organization of independent local Scottish Terrier Specialty clubs; To urge members and breeders to accept the standard of the breed as approved by the American Kennel Club; To do all in its power to protect and advance the interests of the breed and to encourage sportsmanlike competition at dog shows; To conduct sanctioned matches and specialty shows."

At the present time, membership consists of approximately 750 families, all of whom have a strong interest in the breed.

Those applying for membership must complete an application form and have the sponsorship of two STCA members in good standing. In addition, the Code of Ethics, stating that the applicant will follow the ethical standard as set by the STCA board of directors, must be signed. The applicant's name is then published in the national magazine and at the following board meeting, membership will be either approved or denied.

Minimal requirements for membership are:

1. Applicant must have owned a Scottish Terrier for at least two years.

2. Applicant must have been a member of a regional Scottish Terrier club, a local all-breed club, or an obedience club for two years.

3. Applicant must have demonstrated a willingness to accept the Code of Ethics in regard to breeding practices.

With membership in the STCA, a new member will receive the current handbook which contains history, pertinent educational articles and advertisements. He will receive the *Bagpiper*, which is the breed magazine that is published on a quarterly basis. The *Bagpiper*

The national specialty at Montgomery County, 1991. Judge Anne Rogers Clark and handler Tom Natalini. Rain or shine, the show must go on!

will keep a member current on the business at hand and on future activities of the STCA. Even living miles from another STCA member, one can keep up with the news and activities of the Scottie world.

The STCA holds its national specialty show each year on the first weekend of October in Ambler, Pennsylvania. This is held in conjunction with the Montgomery County Kennel Club All-Terrier Show. Entries for Scots range from 125 to over 200 in number. This is the show where the breeders will bring out their top stock, not only to compete, but to give other breeders an opportunity to see what they are producing and the chance to go over each other's dogs.

In addition to the national specialty, the club also holds an annual rotating specialty which moves around the country from one location to another, giving the breeders who are unable to make the trip to Pennsylvania an opportunity to show their dogs to the fancy.

The national club offers approximately 20 awards that a member may work toward, of which the Frances G. Lloyd Memorial trophy is the most prestigious. The other

The national rotating specialty 1991—the Great Western Terrier Show in Pasadena, California. The author is judging.

awards vary from the number of champion get for a stud dog to a junior showmanship award to an award for good sportsmanship.

Working under the authority and guidance of the American Kennel Club and the STCA, there are presently 20 regional clubs throughout the country. Meetings are usually held on a monthly basis. Grooming sessions are presented by the experienced members to help the newcomers, and fun matches are held once or twice a year. Most of these clubs hold their own annual specialties, which are well-attended by fanciers in the area. Many individuals will only belong to the regional club, finding everything that they need within this group. There is often a camaraderie and a willingness to help each other that make these clubs very special, and some members find it worthwhile to drive 150 miles or so to attend a monthly meeting.

Within the STCA, the membership includes those who are actively breeding and showing; those who judge not only the Scottish Terrier but all terriers and dogs in other groups; those who have written about the Scottie and dogs in general; and those who year after year work doggedly behind the scenes taking care of the club's business. A wide range of people whose interest and love for the Scotties bond them together, often forming friendships for a lifetime.

Obedience match of the Scottish Terrier Club of Greater Washington, D.C., 1992. Long down exercise.

For information on the STCA or a regional club, write to the American Kennel Club and they will send you the name and address of the current corresponding secretary. You may also contact your local all-breed club for the locality of a regional club.

A fun match in New Jersey.

THE FRANCIS G. LLOYD MEMORIAL CHALLENGE CUP 1921-1992

RECIPIENTS

1921 Ch. Albourne Beetle, Fairwold Kennels

1922 Ch. Rannoch Moor Cricket, Mr. and Mrs. P. D. Schreiber

1923 Ch. Bentley Cotsol Lassie, Fairwold Kennels

1924 Ch. Bentley Cotsol Lassie, Fairwold Kennels

1925 Mrs. Maurice Newton

1926 Fairwold Kennels

1927 Ch. Laindon Lauds, Miss Mary Ray Winters

1928 Ch. Laindon Lauds, Miss Mary Ray Winters

1929 Ch. Ballantrae Wendy, Ballantrae Kennels

1930 Ch. Ballantrae Wendy, Ballantrae Kennels

1931 Ch. Rookery Repeater of Hitofa, Frank Spiekerman

1932 Ch. Heather Enchantress of Hitofa, Frank Spiekerman

1933 Ch. Heather Reveller of Sporran, S. S. Van Dine

1934 Ch. Ortley Patience of Hollybourne, S. L. Froelich

1935 Ch. Flornell Soundman, Braw Bricht Kennels

1936 Ch. Flornell Soundfella, Relgalf Kennels

1937 Ch. Marlu Milady, Marlu Farm Kennels

1938 Ch. Flornell Sound Laddie, Relgalf Kennels

1939 Ch. Flornell Sound Laddie, Relgalf Kennels

1940 Ch. Bradthorn Bullion, Relgalf Kennels

1941 Ch. Relgalf Ribbon Raider, Relgalf Kennels

1942 Ch. Relgalf Ribbon Raider, Relgalf Kennels

1943 Ch. Relgalf Ribbon Raider, Relgalf Kennels

1944 Ch. Ayerscott Anita, Mr. and Mrs. A. C. Ayers

1945 Ch. Relgalf Rebel Leader, Relgalf Kennels

1946 Ch. Relgalf Rebel Leader, Relgalf Kennels

1947 Ch. Relgalf Rebel Leader, Relgalf Kennels

1948 Ch. Deephaven Red Seal, Marlu Farm Kennels

1949 Ch. Walsing Winning Trick of Edgerstoune, Edgerstoune Kennels

1950 Ch. Gold Finder's Admiral, Mr. and Mrs. Edward Moloney

1951 Ch. Barberry Knowe Barbican, Mr. and Mrs. Charles C. Stalter

1952 Ch. Barberry Knowe Barbican, Mr. and Mrs. Charles C. Stalter

1953 Ch. Lynwood Angus, William R. Wood

1954 Ch. Rebel Invader, Dr. and Mrs. W. Stewart Carter

1955 Ch. Wyrebury Worthwhile, Dr. and Mrs. Joseph A. Thomas

1956 Ch. Cantie Confident, Marguerite Fuller

1957 Ch. Todhill's Cinnamon Bear, Mr. and Mrs. Robert C. Graham

1958 Ch. Westpark Derriford Baffie, Carnation Farm Kennel

1959 Ch. Blanart Bewitching, Blanche E. Reeg

1960 Ch. Blanart Bewitching, Blanche E. Reeg

1961 Ch. Crisscot Carnival, Cornelia M. Crissey

1962 Ch. Walsing Wild Winter of Barberry Knowe, Mr. and Mrs. Charles C. Stalter

1963 Ch. Gaidoune Great Bear, Miss Helen B. Gaither

1964 Ch. Anstamm Dark Venture, Mr. and Mrs. Anthony Stamm

1965 Ch. Gaidoune Grin and Bear It, Miss Helen Gaither

1966 Ch. Bardene Bobby Dazzler, Mr. and Mrs. Anthony Stamm

1967 Ch. Mar De's Dark Felicia, Mr. and Mrs. Edmond P. FitzWilliam

1968 Ch. Balachan Night Hawk, Dr. and Mrs. T. Allen Kirk, Jr.

1969 Ch. Gadiscot Guid Giftie, Mrs. Betty Munden

1970 Ch. Gosmore Eilburn Admaration, Mr. and Mrs. Clive Pillsbury

1971 Ch. Gosmore Eilburn Admaration, Mr. and Mrs. Clive Pillsbury

1972 Ch. Anstamm Happy Venture, Mr. and Mrs. A. Stamm

1973 Ch. Anstamm Happy Venture, Mr. and Mrs. A. Stamm

1974 Ch. Burbury's Sir Lancelot, Linda Catlin

1975 Ch. Sandoone Royal Barclay, Miss Betty Malinka

1976 Ch. Dunbar's Democrat of Sandoone, R. Hensel & Wm. Crouse

1977 Ch. Dunbar's Democrat of Sandoone, R. Hensel & Wm. Crouse

1978 Ch. Anstamm Happy Sonata, Mrs. Miriam Stamm

1979 Ch. Ruff-Me-Tuff Rabble Rouser, Mr. and Mrs. Wm. Shanholtz

1980 Ch. Ruff-Me-Tuff Rabble Rouser, Mr. and Mrs. Wm. Shanholtz

1981 Ch. Democratic Victory, Mr. and Mrs. R. Willis

1982 Ch. Democratic Victory, Mr. and Mrs. R. Willis

1983 Ch. Braeburn's Close Encounter, Mr. and Mrs. A. Novick

1984 Ch. Braeburn's Close Encounter, Mr. and Mrs. A. Novick

1985 Ch. Simonsez Charlie The Charmer, E. Louise Simon

1986 Ch. Sandgreg's Sweet Luv, J & E Boso, B. DeSaye

1987 Ch. Sandgreg's Foxmoor, J & E Boso

1988 Ch. Sandgreg's Foxmoor, J & E Boso

1989 Ch. Anstamm Heat Wave, Anstamm Kennels

1990 Ch. Justscott's Reanda Just Rite, Robert & Jane Phelan

1991 Ch. Brookhill's Morning Edition, Marjorie Carpenter

1992 Ch. Anstamm Low Commotion, Fred and Patty Brooks and Anstamm Kennels.

The Francis G. Lloyd Memorial Challenge Cup.

Ch. Anstamm Heat Wave, whelped 1987, by Ch. Anstamm Summer Lightning ex Gayla's Mercedes Venture. Breeder, Gayla Schaubel. Owner, Anstamm Kennel. Winner of the Lloyd trophy 1989.

The Scottish Terrier Standard

Each breed approved by the American Kennel Club has a standard which gives the reader a mental picture of what the specific breed should look like. This gives breeders and judges a pattern to work from and an ideal to work toward. All reputable breeders strive continually to produce animals that will meet the requirements of the standard.

As with all breed standards, the purpose of the breed, in addition to the overall look of the breed, are considerations when writing the standard. Standards were originally written by fanciers who had a love and a concern for the breed. They knew that the essential characteristics of the Scottish Terrier were unlike any other breed and that care must be taken that these characteristics were maintained through the generations.

Ch. Anstruther's Moffat

The English standard for the Scottish Terrier was used in America until 1925 and then a new American standard was drawn up which did away with the half-prick ear and changed the wording for the neck, placing "moderately" before the word short. The body description was changed from "of moderate length" to "moderately short."

The 1925 standard was used until 1947 and this is the standard that was used until 1993, when the newly reformatted present standard was adopted.The 1947 standard was written by S. Edwin Megargee, Jr., Theodore Bennett, John Kemps and Maurice Pollak, names that are still remembered by those who are considered to be the elders of the breed.

It can be seen that the Scottish Terrier has changed little in conformation over the past 100 years. However, taste and style in grooming have changed over the years and that can give the dog a somewhat different appearance from one generation to another.

In addition to having dogs that *look* like a proper Scottish Terrier, the standard assures that our dogs will have the proper Scottie spirit and, even if the breed may not have been used in the field for years, the dogs will still have the desire and the ability to go to ground and to bring out a rat or a rabbit.

The standard is continually studied by serious dog breeders and by judges. However, the reading and interpretation of the standard is subjective and open to interpretation by the individual who is reading it. To assist the new breeder, the STCA has put together a fine booklet entitled *The Clarification and Amplification of the Scottish Terrier Standard.* When an individual joins the national club, this becomes a part of the information packet that is received.

Ch. Hughcrest Kentucky Brew, owned by Chris and Judy Hughes.

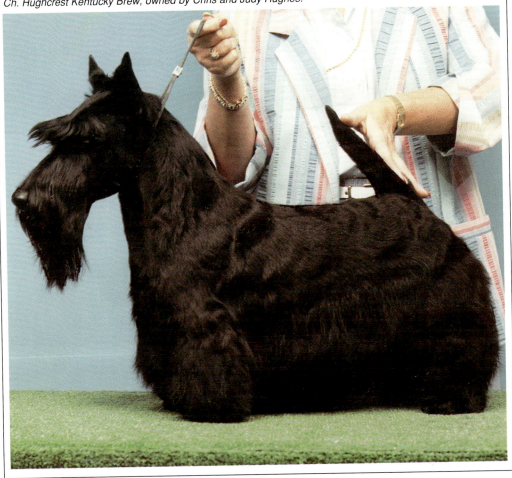

Am., Can. Ch. McVan's Ebony Rose, owned by Vandra L. Huber.

**AMERICAN KENNEL CLUB'S
OFFICIAL BREED STANDARD
Adopted April 8, 1993**

GENERAL APPEARANCE: The Scottish Terrier is a small, compact, short-legged, sturdily-built dog of good bone and substance. His head is long in proportion to his size. He has a hard, wiry, weather-resistant coat and a thick-set, cobby body which is hung between short, heavy legs. These characteristics, joined with his very special keen, piercing, "varminty" expression, and his erect ears and tail, are salient features of the breed. The Scottish Terrier's bold, confident, dignified aspect exemplifies power in a small package.

SIZE, PROPORTION AND SUBSTANCE: The Scottish Terrier should have a thick body and heavy bone. The principal objective must be **symmetry and balance** without exaggeration. Equal consideration should be given to height, weight, length of back and length of head. Height **at withers** for either sex should be **about** 10 inches. The length of back from withers to set-on tail should be approximately 11 inches. Generally, a well-balanced Scottish Terrier dog should weigh from 19 to 22 pounds and a bitch from 18 to 21 pounds.

HEAD: The head should be long in proportion to the overall length and size of the dog. In profile, the skull and muzzle should give the appearance of two parallel planes.

The SKULL should be long and of medium width, slightly domed and covered with short, hard hair. In profile, the skull should **appear** flat. There should be a slight but definite stop between the skull and muzzle at eye level, allowing the eyes to be **set in under the brow,** contributing to proper Scottish Terrier expression. The skull should be smooth with no prominences or depressions and cheeks should be flat and clean.

The MUZZLE should be approximately equal to the length of skull with only a slight taper to the nose. The muzzle should be well filled in under the eye, with no evidence of snipeyness. A correct Scottish Terrier muzzle should fill an average man's hand.

The NOSE should be black, regardless of coat color, and of good size, projecting somewhat over the mouth and giving the impression that the upper jaw is longer than the lower one.

The TEETH should be large and evenly spaced, having either a scissor or level bite, the former preferred. The jaw should be square, level and powerful. Undershot or overshot bites should be penalized

The EYES should be set wide apart and well in under the brow. They should be small, bright and piercing, and almond-shaped, not round. The color should be dark brown or nearly black, the darker the better.

The EARS should be small, prick, set well up on the skull and pointed, but never cut. They should be covered with short velvety hair. From the front, the outer edge of the ear should form a straight line up from the side of the skull. The use, size, shape and placement of the ear and its erect carriage are major elements of the keen, alert, intelligent Scottish Terrier expression.

NECK, TOPLINE, BODY:

The NECK should be **moderately** short, strong, thick and muscular, blending smoothly into well laid back shoulders. The neck must never be so short as to appear clumsy.

The BODY should be **moderately** short with ribs extending well back into a short, strong loin, deep flanks and very muscular hindquarters. The ribs should be well sprung out from the spine, forming a broad, strong back, then curving down and inward to form a deep body that would be nearly heart-shaped if viewed in cross-section.

The TOPLINE of the back should be firm and level.

The CHEST should be broad, very deep and well let down between the forelegs. The forechest should extend well in front of the legs and drop well down into the brisket. The chest should not be flat or concave, and the brisket should nicely fill an average man's slightly-cupped hand. The lowest point of the brisket should be such that an average man's fist would fit under it with little or no overhead clearance.

The TAIL should be about seven inches long and never cut. It should be set on high and carried erectly, either vertical or with a slight curve forward, but not over the back. The tail should be thick at the base, tapering gradually to a point and covered with short, hard hair.

FOREQUARTERS: The shoulders should be well laid back and moderately well knit at the withers. The forelegs should be very heavy in bone, straight or slightly bent with elbows close to the body, and set in under the shoulder blade with a definite forechest in front of them. Scottish Terriers should not be out at the elbows.

The FOREFEET should be larger than the hind feet, round thick and compact with strong nails. The front feet should point straight ahead, but a **slight** "toeing out" is acceptable. Dew claws may be removed.

HINDQUARTERS: The thighs should be very muscular and powerful for the size of the dog with the stifles well bent and the legs straight from the hock to heel. Hocks should be well let down and parallel to each other.

COAT: The Scottish Terrier should have a broken coat. It is a hard, wiry outer coat with a soft, dense undercoat. The coat should be trimmed and blended into the furnishings to give a distinct Scottish Terrier outline. The dog should be presented with sufficient coat so that the texture and density may be determined. The longer coat on the beard, legs and lower body may be slightly softer than the body coat but should not be or appear fluffy.

COLOR: Black, wheaten or brindle of any color. Many black and brindle dogs have sprinklings of white or silver hairs in their coats which are normal and not to be penalized. White can be allowed only on the chest and chin and that to a slight extent only.

GAIT: The gait of the Scottish Terrier is very characteristic of the breed. It is not the square trot or walk desirable in the long-legged breeds. The forelegs do not move in exact parallel planes; rather, in reaching out, the forelegs incline **slightly** inward because of the deep broad forechest. Movement should be free, agile and coordinated with powerful drive from the rear and good reach in front. The action of the rear legs should be square and true and, at the trot, both the hocks and stifles should be flexed with a vigorous motion. When the dog is in motion, the back should remain firm and level.

TEMPERAMENT: The Scottish Terrier should be alert and spirited but also stable and steady-going. He is a determined and thoughtful dog whose "heads up, tails up" attitude in the ring should convey both fire and control. The Scottish Terrier, while loving and gentle with people, can be aggressive with other dogs. He should exude ruggedness and power, living up to his nickname, the "Diehard."

PENALTIES: Soft coat; curly coat; round, protruding or light eyes; overshot or undershot jaws; obviously oversize or undersize; shyness or timidity; upright shoulders; lack of reach in front or drive in rear; stiff or stilted movement; movement too wide or too close in rear; too narrow in front or rear; out at the elbow; lack of bone and substance; low set tail; lack of pigment in the nose; coarse head; and failure to show with head and tail up are faults to be penalized

NO JUDGE SHOULD PUT TO WINNERS OR BEST OF BREED ANY SCOTTISH TERRIER NOT SHOWING REAL TERRIER CHARACTER IN THE RING.

SCALE OF POINTS

Skull	5
Muzzle	5
Eyes	5
Ears	10
Neck	5
Chest	5
Body	15
Legs and Feet	10
Tail	5
Coat	15
Size	10
Appearance	10
Total	100

INTERPRETATION AND ILLUSTRATION OF THE STANDARD
Drawings by Marion Krupp

The overall picture should be of a sturdy, compact, muscular dog—a dog that is low to the ground with four sturdy legs under him and with an upright tail like a rudder. His head should be long and lean with keen eyes and small upright ears. He should portray power in a small package and should possess a willingness to work. He must be a well-balanced dog that moves like he could do a day's work in what he was bred to do. His body parts must fit together so that he can move and work in the most efficient and tireless way possible.

We will now take the standard point by point. The correct type is a dog that is low to the ground. Bodywise, he will present a picture of a fairly square dog with a "shoe box" for a head. He must not appear taller than his length and he should not be excessively exaggerated in any area.

The head, which covers the skull, muzzle, eyes, and ears, makes up 25% of the standard.

The skull should be long and lean and in proportion to the body of the dog. It should be of medium width and slightly domed, leaving room for brain power. You should not feel any bumps or protrusions from the cheek bones when going over the head as this will give a "cheeky" appearance. Viewed from the side, the top plane of the skull will run parallel to the plane of the muzzle.

The muzzle should be in proportion to the length of the skull, either the same length or slightly longer and there should be a slight stop, which is a drop between the skull and the foreface, just in front of the eye. There should be no indication of snipiness. The jaw bone should be square, leaving ample room for the teeth. The teeth should have a scissors bite, neither overshot nor undershot.

The correct eye will give the Scot the keen, varminty look that is so essential to the breed. The standard says it all.

The ears must be set well up on the skull and should be rather small. Ears that are carried wide to the side, that are excessively large or have a "bat-like" look are not to be encouraged in any way.

Moving along the body, the neck, chest and body make up 30% of the standard. The neck is to be moderately short, thick and muscular, set correctly on sloping shoulders.

The chest must be broad and deep. It should be wide enough so that you can place your hand, palm up, under the chest and the dog should not have to move either leg for you to do this. The chest should fill your hand. If you make a fist and place it between the chest and the table that your dog is standing on, your fist should fit under the dog without too much clearance.

The shoulders are well laid back (sloping) with the correct angulation. An animal who does not have this correct angulation will have a weak or loaded (heavy) shoulder. Consequently he will be out-at-the-elbows, a decided fault. A dog with the incorrect shoulder placement will not move correctly, often presenting a picture of "paddling" with his front legs as he moves toward you.

The body is "moderately short and well ribbed up with strong loins, deep flanks and very muscular hindquarters." Note the words used—strong, deep, muscular. Bred well, the Scottish Terrier will never resemble a toy dog. This is a substantial animal even if it is only 10 inches or so in height.

The loin is short and strong with a close coupling between the front and hindquarters, presenting a compact dog. The topline should be level from the shoulders to the set-on of the tail. There should not be a dip behind the withers.

The tail must be well set with a slight curve. It should be carried properly, not gaily over the back or sagging between the legs.

The legs and feet are short and heavy in bone. Stifles are well bent and the thighs are very muscular. The front legs are allowed to be slightly bent to allow room for the chest, but he must not be out at the elbows. Again as in the front quarters, the rear legs should be well angulated with the feet placed squarely under the legs. The feet should be thick and round and the forefeet will be larger than the rear feet. Remember that this is an animal whose purpose is to go to ground and dig out small animals. Strong legs and feet with the correct body placement are essentials.

The gait of the Scottie is described well in the standard. He should display strong, free movement and move with conviction.

The standard calls for a rather short coat of two inches or so in length. This is a double-coated dog and he will carry a dense undercoat with a hard and wiry outercoat.

The Scottish Terrier should be about ten inches high at the shoulder and his weight will be anywhere from 18 to 22 pounds. Some Scots will be bigger, some smaller, and the males, in general, will be larger and heavier than the females.

The standard states that "the principal objective must be symmetry and balance," and this is a factor that all breeders must keep in mind.

The colors of the breed are numerous, with the basic colors being black, brindle and wheaten. Within the last two colors there can be a wide range of shades. Brindles can be brown, red, gray or silver. Wheatens run from light golden, the color of wheat, to red. All colors are permissible except for white, which is an unacceptable color in the breed.

The general appearance, as stated in the standard, is to give the impression of immense power in a small size.

T. W. Hancock Mountjoy wrote in his book *Points of the Dog,* "In general appearance he should be short-backed, deep-chested, low to the ground and stockily built, with a good spring of rib and cobby body. Although he has very short legs, he should have good action with no stiltiness; being out of shoulder is a great fault. His feet should be strong and thick; the coat should be very hard, harsh and wiry; the head long, with a very slight stop between the eyes; the muzzle powerful with a good length. Teeth should be level; nose black; ears very small and pricked; the neck short and very muscular and set on sloping shoulders. The eye should be very bright and rather sunken which gives the "varminty" expression. Hindquarters should be well developed, and the tail should be carried gaily and be about six inches long." This description was written over 60 years ago and it still holds true today.

Puppy from Stonehedge Kennel.

Su-et's Disney Girl, dam of Ch. Deblin's Small Talk.

Characteristics of the Scottish Terrier

Scottish Terriers in the past have been called "The Diehard" and "The Aberdeen" but for many years now they have been known by the general public as "The Scottie." "Do you have a white one or a black one?" they will ask. A short explanation can educate these individuals that the "white one" is the West Highland White Terrier, a dog that is smaller in size than a Scottie, possesses a shorter muzzle and is always white in color. The Scottie, like his fellow countryman, tends to be a rather dour, sober fellow who knows that life is serious and that it is to be met with dignity.

Scotties have been described in many ways and all the names fit the breed: lion-hearted, robust, alert, curious, scrappy, bright-eyed, intelligent, sturdy, courageous and adaptable. This is a breed with pluck and intelligence. They are sensitive to both criticism and praise. They are adaptable and if given good food, a bed and love, they can adjust to almost any living condition with little difficulty. This is a below-the-knee dog that is long on gameness, determination and courage. In no way can it be regarded as a toy dog. It has been said that a Scottie is a dog that "can go anywhere and do anything."

Common characteristics for all terriers are their desire to work with great enthusiasm and courage. They all have large and powerful teeth for the size of their bodies; they have keen hearing and excellent eyesight. No matter for how many generations they have been pets, the purpose for which the breed was bred will remain with the dog.

The temperament of the Scottish

Ch. Charthill Royal Stewart and Ch. Colwick Prime Time eagerly await Tom and Charla Hill's arrival home.

Terrier is all terrier. He is quick, alert, intelligent and robust. The Scot, however, is a bit less rambunctious than other terrier breeds. He can have a tendency to be a one-man, or more particularly, one-family dog. He likes attention but doesn't want to be overwhelmed. He will sit or lay next to you but he may not want to sit on your lap. He enjoys a good game or a giggle with his master, but he doesn't like to be made fun of. Always laugh with him and not at him.

He is sensitive to praise and to blame. He can adjust easily to children, but children must understand his independent nature and his sense of dignity. Unlike a Golden Retriever, this is not a pet to be hauled around, have his ears pulled or to be ridden upon. He enjoys walks with his family, a toss of the tennis ball to be retrieved, and quiet nights by the fire. He will ask little of you but a bit of love and some conversation.

The Scottish Terrier has a tendency to be a bit stubborn. They are independent, with minds of their own, and they obey grudgingly and at their own speed. They can quickly figure out what is expected of them and just as quickly work their way around your expectations. They have proven to be a challenge for those who work with them in obedience, thus you will not see as many Scottie obedience champions as in some other terrier breeds. Scottie owners who work their dogs in obedience often feel that their dog may not have

Scots sniffing flowers!—a day in the garden.

achieved the title of companion dog, but that they themselves have learned a great deal of humility.

Scotties are basically no-nonsense dogs. They will not stand in the yard and bark for hours as some breeds will and they will usually bark only when they hear a noise and want to alert their owners. The Scottie is a natural-born fighter. He will stand his ground but his actions will usually be defensive, protecting his territory as a sentinel.

A no-nonsense Scottie pup in her Easter bonnet.

S. S. Van Dyne, a famous mystery writer and breeder of Scottish Terriers, wrote: "A gentleman! This is perhaps the whole story. The Scottie is a gentleman. He is reserved, honorable, patient, tolerant and courageous. He doesn't annoy you or force himself upon you. He meets life as he finds it, with an instinctive philosophy, a stoical intrepidy and a mellow understanding. He is calm and firm, and he minds his own business—and minds it well. He is a Spartan and can suffer pain without whimpering, which is more than the majority of human beings can do. He will attack a lion or a tiger if his rights are invaded, and though he may die in the struggle he never shows the white feather or runs away. He is the most admirable of all sports, forthright, brave and uncomplaining. You know exactly where you stand with a Scottie; and if you are a friend, he is gentle, loving and protective."

Who can resist a young Scottie like this one?

Buying Your Scottish Terrier

It must be remembered that when you purchase a pet, be it a cat or a dog, the animal will become a part of your family and will probably be with you from five to 15 years. Unlike your brothers or sisters, when you elect to bring home a pet you get to select the one that you think will fit into the family the best, the pet who will be a welcome addition to your family's style of living.

Buying a dog should require some study and some time. Do not rush out to the pet shop and bring home the dog that looks the neediest; do not run out to your neighbor who breeds her bitch every six months to the male down the block; do not bring home a puppy that grows into a 100-pound dog and no longer fits into your two room apartment. And for heaven's sake, do not buy the puppy that hangs back in the box because you feel sorry for him. When you add this member to the family, take a good look at what you are buying and make certain that this is what your family wants and needs.

Consider the purchase of your dog as a major purchase. You may take six months or so to select your new car or a major appliance. Take at least that long to select your dog. You may have the car for five years but your puppy will become a family member for the years of his life, and that will probably be at least eight years and may be as much as 12 or 15 years. And as they say, having a dog is just like having a child, except it never grows up.

The next step that you should take is to attend a local all-breed dog show and watch the Scottish Terrier judging. Look over your catalog and see who the breeders are and from which kennels the winners are coming. After the judging, talk to these breeders and ask any questions that you still have in regard to Scottie ownership.

Throughout this book we have referred to "reputable" breeders. A reputable breeder is one who is devoted to making certain that you and the Scottish Terrier are suited to each other. He will want to know that you will offer a good home life, including a fenced-in yard and the attention and the love that the dog will need. A reputable breeder has carefully selected his breeding animals and is continually striving to produce better dogs. He has checked the health of his puppies, wormed them, given them their shots and has done his best not to have bred in any genetic problems. A reputable breeder will sell you a Scot that *looks* like a Scot and has the proper temperament.

A reputable breeder will belong to a local all-breed club, a regional Scottish Terrier club or to the national club. Do not hesitate to ask the breeder which organizations he

The Easter bunny in the shape of a puppy from Ashmoor Kennel

A handful of Scottie

"Now, this is cute" from Sparwyn Kennel.

A young Wheaten giving serious consideration to life.

Above: If you are fortunate, you may be able to visit your new Scottish Terrier puppy when he's only three or four weeks old. Observing the development over the first six weeks is most fascinating.

Below: Playing with young pups is a vital part of socialization. Be sure your new acquisition is playful, alert and fearless.

117

belongs to, how active he has been and how long he has been a member.

When you visit a kennel, look around and see that it is clean and cared for. The yard should be clean, the kennel area well lit and the puppies should be fat and happy. They should enjoy seeing a stranger and not cower in a corner. The breeder should show you the dam of the litter and if the sire is on the premises, you will also be shown the sire. These dogs should be in good condition, healthy and with good temperaments.

A reputable breeder may not have a puppy for you when you are ready to buy one. Often, breeders only have one or two litters a year and you may have to wait until the next breeding. A reputable breeder will not push a six-week-old puppy on you, but will keep the pup until it is ten or 12 weeks old and ready to leave its nest. Scotties are slow to develop and need time for social adjustment. Because of their short legs they will not be nearly as active at four weeks of age as an Airedale Terrier. Just be patient and the right puppy for you will come your way.

Give some consideration as to whether or not you want a male or a female. A female will come into season every six months or so, unless you have her spayed. Females seem to mature more quickly than the males and with their first season they quickly become young ladies and lose some of the puppy giggles. Males can remain rambunctious teenagers for a long time.

Remember that the coat color of a Scot is black, brindle or wheaten. Do not say, "I will only have a black dog" until you understand the coat colors.

Do not have a closed mind to an older dog. Some kennels will have a two or three year old that they would like to place. There are many advantages to this—the dog is mature, it is often housetrained and if not, it is a quick learner. The mature dog will not chew the rugs and will be well socialized. Sometimes these dogs are champions and the breeder is primarily concerned with finding a good home and has less interest in the price of the dog.

Do not buy your dog from a puppy mill (individuals who may be breeding as many as 100 dogs of various breeds). Puppy mills will often charge as much for a pup as a reputable breeder. However, you are very apt to get a sickly puppy, and worse, one that does not look much like a Scottish Terrier.

If you are a first-time Scottish Terrier owner and have never shown a dog, do expect the breeder to sell you a good dog with a good pedigree, but do not expect that you will receive an animal that will go best in show its first time out. It's always possible, of course, just as possible as winning the super lottery, and your chances will be just about the same. You are looking for a pet, a family member. And for your first dog that is just what the breeder will sell you: A well-bred, healthy, well-adjusted puppy that your family will enjoy for many years.

Wheatens at play.

Scotties are known for their curiosity and friskiness—they need to explore everything.

Above: *Wheaten pup enjoying the sights and smells of the great outdoors.*

Below: *Out for a run with mom—your breeder allows plenty of socialization time for the pups to learn the ropes from their dam.*

Above: Let us all bow our heads in prayer. Owner, Alan Cartwright.

Below: Curiosity gets these McVan wheatens.

Above: Getting ready for Christmas.

Below: Waiting for Santa.

If you are planning to show your Scottie, AKC classes begin as early as six months. It's never too early to start accustoming the pup to the routine of stacking and inspection.

The lovely best in show-winning wheaten Ch. Sandgreg's Sweet Luv by Sandgreg's Square Deal ex Sandgreg's Kismet. Breeders, Charles and Susan Martin. Owners, James and Betty Boso and Barbara DeSaye. Handler, Mark George.

Coat Colors of the Scottish Terrier

Scottish Terriers come in three basic coat colors: black, brindle and wheaten. The general public often assumes that all Scots are black and when picking out a puppy they will insist, "I will only have a black Scottie."

The American Kennel Club registration application lists the following six colors:

Black	Silver brindle
Brindle	Black brindle
Wheaten	Red brindle

The definition of brindle is applied loosely to all coats that are not one self-color throughout. When two colors are listed, the first color is the dominant color. Thus, a black and (with) brindle Scot will often look like a black Scot to a novice as the primary color is black. A gray and brindle will often be called a silver brindle. The wheaten should be the color of golden wheat or ripe corn. All colors are acceptable except white.

Puppy owners should be aware of the color range and know that there is no difference in the Scot underneath the coat, even if the outer coats are of a different color. Some breeders prefer a black dog as this can look very sharp in the ring. Others prefer a brindle coat as sometimes this can be a easier coat to work. And in recent years, the wheaten color has come into great favor with many breeders. The blacks and brindles are the original colors and the wheatens evolved at a later date.

Dr. Fayette Ewing, an early booster and breeder of the Scot, felt

A classic black Scot, Ch. Deblin's Double Dare, whelped 1988, by Ch. Deblin's Back Talk ex Ch. Deblin's Double Talk. Breeders, Deborah Brookes and Lynn Struck. Owners, Deborah and Anthony Brookes.

Eng. Ch. Medwal Miss Mustard was the first wheaten champion in England in four decades. She was whelped in 1948.

and decided that the color of a Scottish Terrier is determined by a pattern of multiple genes rather than a single pair. He came to the conclusion that a solid color (Mrs. Caspersz noted that there are three absolute self-colors in the breed: black, red and wheaten) is recessive to a brindle. Dr. Kirk also suggested the possibility of a second pair of genes which determines the actual color which will dominate the coat. He also thought that there was a possibility of a third pair of genes that determines what the second color of a brindle dog will be.

There is still room for research in the area of colors for a formula as to how colors are determined. What is known is that specific dogs have been prepotent in passing along certain genes for producing a tendency for certain colors.

The Glencannie Kennels in England bred a dog called Ch. Glencannie Red Robin. Mrs. Caspersz wrote: "A grandly made dog, combining substance and quality and possessed of a lovely outline." He was prepotent for light colors, and sired the light gray English Ch. Reimill Realist and the light red brindle English Ch. Brantvale Boilin' O'er. The key dog in Red Robin's pedigree was English Ch. Heather Necessity. Through his son, Lambley Sandboy, came the Medwal wheatens.

Mr. W. Medwal of England had

that the lighter colors should be considered as well as the blacks and brindles. His first wheaten import was Loyne Ginger and his second import was English Ch. Ems Morning Nip, whelped in 1908. Nip was described as a "bright golden brindle, with a coat the shade of ripe corn, flecked with black hairs."

The original Scots were primarily of the brindle shadings and occasionally in the early days, there would be a white patch on the chest. On rare occasions one will still see a small white blaze on the chest of a dog being shown. Puppies born with tufts of white on their chin or chest will lose these markings as they mature.

During the 1920s there was a surge of interest in the all-black dog, partly because the well-known winners Ch. Albourne Admiration and Ch. Heather Necessity were black.

Dr. T. Allen Kirk researched the genetic possibilities of coat colors been active in Scots for many years. In 1947 their first home-bred champion appeared, English Ch. Medwal Miss Mustard. Between Ch. Ems Morning Nip in 1908 and Miss Mustard in 1947, there had been light-colored and silver-gray champions in England but no wheaten champions. Miss Mustard did much to revive the wheaten color in the breed. Mrs. Caspersz wrote: "Not only is she brilliant in colour, with her body coat the

Ch. Carnation Golden Girl was the first all-breed best in show wheaten Scot. Owners, Carnation Farm Kennels. Handler, Bob Bartos.

shade of ripe corn and slightly darker tints suggestive of autumn leaves on her head, legs and tail, but her disposition is as sunny as her coat . . ."

In America, Deephaven Kennels imported the 11-month-old brindle Heather Asset, eventual sire of 16 champions, and he became a dominating influence in the wheaten Scotties through his non-wheaten get. Marie Stone of Kinclaven Kennels became well known for her wheatens, finishing Kinclaven Wild Oats and Kinclaven Winter Wheat in 1945.

Deephaven Spade Flush sired Ch. Carnation Golden Girl in 1950. Handled by Bob Bartos, Golden Girl was the first wheaten to go best in show until 1985, when Ch. Sandgreg's Sweet Luv achieved top honors.

Mrs. W. M. Robertson from Glad Mac Kennels in Washington produced many winning wheatens during the 1950s. Her foundation stock came from Ch. Reimill Radiator and Deephaven Spade Flush. Ch. Glad Mac's Rolling Stone sired 16 champions. Mrs. Robertson later owned the group-winning Ch. Sandgreg's Hot Shot and the black dog Ch. Sandgreg's Square Deal.

Square Deal is now the sire of 34 champions, including the record-breaking wheaten bitch trio of Ch. Sandgreg's Sweet Luv, best in show wheaten bitch; Ch. Wychwyre Liberty, the first wheaten to go Winners Bitch at Montgomery County; and Ch. Sandgreg's Sweet Charity, another top-winner. All three bitches were out of Ch. Sandgreg's Kismet.

John and Barbara DeSaye of

Ch. Wychwyre Liberty, whelped 1981, by Sandgreg's Square Deal ex Ch. Sandgreg's Kismet, was the dam of ten champions, including four specialty winners. Owner-breeders, Bill and Sue Martin.

Sandgreg Kennels have revolutionized the wheaten dogs through their breeding program. The daughters of Ch. Sandgreg's Editorial bred to Ch. Sandgreg's Square Deal have produced top-winning wheatens. By bringing the Firebrand line into their original program of Glad Mac and

Am., Can. Ch. Sandgreg's Sweet Charity, whelped 1980, by Square Deal ex Kismet, is the dam of 11 champions. Owners, John and Barbara DeSaye.

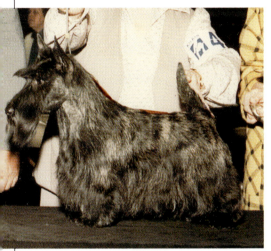

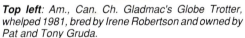

Top left: Am., Can. Ch. Gladmac's Globe Trotter, whelped 1981, bred by Irene Robertson and owned by Pat and Tony Gruda.
Top right: Ch. Hughcrest Sparkling Burgundy, bred by Judy Hughes and Marge Drake, owned by Chris and Judy Hughes.
Middle left: Ch. Ruff Me Tuff Royal Stuff, bred by Jake and Nancy McClosky, owned by Ruth Ann Krause.
Middle right: Am., Can. Ch. Barraglen's Bachelor's Bait, whelped 1980, bred and owned by Kathleen and Ann Bower.
Bottom right: Ch. Charthill Victory at Sea, whelped 1990, bred by Richard and Victoria Lapishka and owned by Charla Hill.

Int. Ch. McVan's Sandman belongs to Dr. Vandra Huber.

Gilkey, wheatens were brought to a quality where they would do top winning throughout the country.

Barbara DeSaye has done considerable research on the wheaten and I would like to quote from her article in the 1986 STCA handbook:

"It is generally assumed that the gene for wheaten color is recessive. In order for the color to manifest itself the dog must carry two genes for wheaten color. For example, the sire or dam itself may be black or brindle, but will have the ability to pass a wheaten color gene to its offspring if it possesses that gene. If the other parent is also able to pass a wheaten color gene, that is if it is a heterozygous black or a homozygous wheaten, wheaten offspring can be produced."

Remember when purchasing your Scottish Terrier: If you are purchasing your first Scottie, keep an open mind to color. Black and all the shades of brindle and wheaten are equally desirable. The most important factor in your purchase is that you are buying a well-bred, healthy pup who has a disposition that you like. Breeding . . . disposition . . . health . . . these are the factors that should be considered before coat color preference.

Grooming the Scottish Terrier

Do understand before purchasing your Scottish Terrier that this is a breed with a coat that needs maintenance, whether you have a dog for the show ring or one that is a household pet. Think of it in terms of your child—you bathe your youngster, comb his hair and put a clean set of clothes on him. The end product is that you have a child that smells good, looks nice, and that you enjoy having in your company. It is the same with your dog—keep the dog brushed, cleaned and trimmed and you will find it a pleasure to be in his company. However, it will require some effort to do this.

The Scottie is a double-coated dog. There is a dense, thick undercoat that protects the dog in all kinds of weather and there is a harsh outercoat. Coat care for the pet Scottie can be much different and easier than the coat care for a show dog. The vast majority of Scottie fanciers has a dog for a pet and they should not expect to maintain a show coat.

I found the following advice in The Scottish Terrier by Holland Buckley, London, 1913. This is the complete chapter for "Bathing and Grooming":

"Most people wash their dogs regularly. Unless preparing a puppy for a special purpose, do not bathe him at all, at least not artificially, but get him used to swimming in a pond or the river, never forgetting to give him a good gallop and a rub down afterwards.

"By this system your puppy will be free from colds and kindred ailments. Use disinfectants and soaps in your kennels and in cleaning feeding vessels.

"A few minutes spent each day

Deblin Scot ready and waiting to enter the ring.

131

Last minute touch up.

ing for the show is an art, and an art that cannot be learned in a few months. Furthermore, it is very difficult but not impossible to learn it from a book.

We will take several scenarios for learning to groom for the show:

1. You purchase your pup from a breeder who lives an easy driving distance from your home. Once a month or so, you will spend a three- or four-hour session with her learning how to achieve a coat for the show ring. She will show you how to strip and trim your pup. She will send you home with an assignment to work on that you are to have ready when you come for your next session with your dog.

2. You live in a remote area and have no help with a show coat. The best book to help you is published by the STCA, and it is called *A Guide to Grooming the Scottish Terrier* by Merle Taylor. It is inexpensive and the instructions are clear and easy to follow.

with a comb and dandy brush will keep the coat in tip-top condition, and the skin supple and healthy."

If it only were so easy!

THE SHOW COAT

If you are planning to show your Scottish Terrier, you will be ahead of the game if you purchase your puppy from a reputable breeder who grooms and shows her dogs. If so, this is the individual to see for grooming lessons to learn how to get your dog ready for the show ring. Groom-

The primary difference between the pet and show Scottie coat is that the show Scottie will have a dense undercoat and on top of it he will have a shiny, harsh coat that will fit him like a jacket. With the proper coat, the dog presents a smartness in the ring that can be hard to beat.

This coat can only be acquired by stripping the body coat with a stripping knife or by hand. Within ten to 12 weeks, and with the proper upkeep, he will have grown from his "underwear" outfit stage into a smart new outfit ready for the ring. This all takes skill, time and interest to do it well.

GROOMING THE PET SCOT

Pet grooming is different from grooming for the show ring as you use a clipper on the body and scissors for trimming the furnishings. You will not have the harsh, tight-fitting jacket of the show Scot, but you will have a neat, clean and trimmed dog that will still look like a Scottish Terrier. Even those with kennels who are active in the show ring will clip their old dogs or those who are no longer being shown.

Grooming the pet can be an easy job and it can be easily learned by the average pet owner. If you have no interest in this, you should be able to find a pet groomer in your area who will trim the dog for you. You will take your dog in every six to eight weeks, they will clip and bathe him and you will always have a tidy pet around.

Here are the tools that you will need if you are going to do your own grooming:

1. A grooming table, something sturdy with a rubber mat covering the top. You will need a grooming arm (or a "hanger"). You can use a table in your laundry room with an eye hook in the ceiling for holding the leash.

Your dog will now be comfortable even if confined and you will be able to use both hands to work on the dog. Grooming is a very difficult and frustrating job if you try to groom without a table and a grooming arm.

2. A metal comb, a slicker brush, a good, sharp pair of scissors and a toenail trimmer.

3. Electric clippers with a #10 blade.

To Start: Set your dog on the table and put the leash around his neck. Have your leash up behind the ears and have the leash taut when you

fasten it to your eye hook. Do not walk away and leave your dog unattended as he can jump off the table and be left dangling from the leash with his feet scrambling around in the air. (This gives your dog a very "long" neck!)

If this is the first grooming session for your puppy, work only for five or ten minutes at a session. Keep this "fun" for you and for the dog. Never work so long that you both get frustrated and angry.

Take your slicker brush and brush out the entire coat. Brush the whiskers toward the nose, the body hair toward the tail, the tail up toward the tip of the tail. Brush the leg furnishings up toward the body and brush the chest hair down toward the table. Hold the dog up by the front legs and gently brush the stomach hair, first toward the head and then back toward the rear. Watch it on the males! For cleanliness, you may want to take your scissors and trim the area around the penis—carefully. With the girls, trim some of the hair around the vulva.

Now that your dog is brushed out, comb through the coat with your metal comb. By now you have removed a fair amount of dead hair and your dog will already be looking better. You may find some small mats and these can be worked out with your fingers or your comb. If you have not groomed in some time (for shame!) you may have to take your scissors and split a mat or two. However, if you brush your dog out every week or so, you will not have a problem.

We are now at the stage where you will take your clippers in hand. Your dog will only need to be clipped every three months or so, but you may want to touch up the head more often. Lie the clippers flat on the body of the head—try not to gouge into the coat or skin.

Start with the head and follow this pattern:

Note the tufts left between the ears. Note the eyebrows—this is what gives the Scottie his "look." Chop the eyebrows off short and you will have the look of a Schnauzer.

Take your clippers and clip the neck, shoulders, and body, following this pattern. Trim in the direction that the hair lays.

Take your comb and comb the leg hair down toward the table. Take your scissors and trim the legs neatly.

Your dog should now look like a Scottish Terrier. Take your scissors and trim off anything that "sticks out." If this is your first experience,

Grooming illustrations by Marion Krupp.

you may be a bit clumsy, but the hair will grow back in short time. The finished product may not be quite what you had expected, but expertise will come with experience and you will soon be very proud of your efforts.

Put your dog in the laundry tub when you are finished and give him a good bath and rinsing. After toweling him down, return him to the by following the pattern that is already set in the coat. If the coat totally grows out before you start to groom, the pattern will be lost and then you will have to start over again. Just remember, many pet owners can do a much better job trimming their dogs than some professional groomers.

You now have a Scottish Terrier that you can be proud of! When the

grooming table and trim the toenails on all four legs. At this point you can dry your dog with a hair dryer and brush him out again. Or, you can let him dry naturally and then brush him out.

If you have grooming problems, you can take your dog to the professional groomer the first time or two for his grooming. The groomer will "set" the pattern and then it will be easier for you to get the Scottie look two of you walk down the street, watch the attention and admiration that you will attract!

To wrap it up: Your pet should be brushed weekly and bathed as needed. Trim the toenails every month or so and plan to clip the dog every three months. Follow this plan and your dog will be clean, he will have a new "dress" every three months and he will look like a Scottish Terrier.

Be sure to clip your Scottie's toenails monthly, or more often if necessary. Handler, France Bergeron of Quebec. Photography by Isabelle Francais.

Ch. Brookhill's Morning Edition looking for the judge.

The Scottish Terrier in the Show Ring

Dog shows have been in existence in America for well over one-hundred years. The Westminster Kennel Club dog show, held every year in the beginning of February in New York City, is the second oldest annual sporting event in the country, with only the Kentucky Derby having greater longevity. The first Westminster show was held in 1877. In 1911 Scottish Terrier Ch. Tickle 'Em Jock was Best in Show over an entry of 2,000. Jock was the first of six outstanding Scots who have now attained this highest of honors at America's most prestigious dog show.

Dog shows and dog show competitions are not for everyone, but if you are intent on becoming an active breeder you will have to be out at the shows, either showing your own dogs or having them shown by a professional handler.

I attended my first match show in 1964 with an Old English Sheepdog, encouraged by a friend who was showing a Great Dane. Four hundred dogs were crammed into a little building. I thought that everyone was crazy but I was intrigued. Several months later I attended my second show . . . the Minneapolis Kennel Club's annual all-breed bench show. "This," I thought, "is what a dog show is about! Fifteen hundred dogs sitting on benches, wide aisles, breeders and spectators exchanging stories and pedigrees." My third show was in Iowa, and I rode with a friend who had recently purchased a St. Bernard. We didn't know about dog crates, so my OES rode loose in the rear of the station wagon, his wife and I sat in the midsection and my friend drove with the Saint sitting next to him on the front seat. The

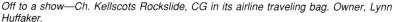
Off to a show—Ch. Kellscots Rockslide, CG in its airline traveling bag. Owner, Lynn Huffaker.

wife travelled the 300-mile trip with a whisk broom in her hand and hit the Saint on the head every time he tried to climb over the seat to go after the OES in the rear. The weather was cold and the show was held in a cow barn. This was not an easy beginning to the sport of showing dogs!

If you are new to the show ring, do attend a few local shows without the ring. The local club will hold one or two seminars a year on grooming for the show ring in addition to having match shows where you can learn how to show your dog. Match shows are run like a dog show, but they are casual and a good place for the beginner to learn. You will not receive any points toward a championship, but you will find out how a dog show is run,

Scots, like all other terriers, are sparred in the ring to show their true terrier spirit.

your dog to see what the game is about. If you are competitive, have the time and the money to compete, and of course have a good dog, this may be the sport and hobby for you.

If you have not already done so, join your local Scottish Terrier club. This is really a must for a novice in and will learn what will be expected of you and your dog. Entry fees at matches are minimal. This is also a good opportunity to meet the people in the breed.

Contact your local all-breed club and find out if they offer conformation classes and start attending these classes on a regular basis. One class does not an expert make! Your all-breed club will hold one or two matches a year and you should plan to attend these matches.

When you think that you are ready . . . your dog is in coat and can walk on a lead, and you feel a tiny bit of confidence, enter an AKC-licensed dog show.

Dog shows are divided into seven Groups of dogs, of which the Terriers are the fourth Group following the Sporting, Hound and Working Groups. The Terriers are followed by the Toys, Non-Sporting and Herding Groups.

You will enter your dog as a Scottish Terrier as either a dog (male) or a bitch (female). Unless your dog is a champion, you must enter the class for puppy six- to 12-month, 12- to 18-month, Novice, American-bred (no imports), Bred-by-Exhibitor (you are listed as the breeder of the dog) or Open. If you are inexperienced, you may want to consider the American-bred or 12-18-month class if your dog is no longer eligible for the puppy class. Enter your dog in the Open class when the two of you can work as a team and your confidence is in hand.

The judge will place each class first, second, third and fourth. Each class winner will then compete for winners dog and winners bitch. After the non-champion dogs and

Best in show trophies come in all shapes, sizes and styles. Winning the Indianhead KC in 1987 is Ch. Firebrands's Sunday Scherzo handled by John Sheehan. The author happily looks on.

In the ring, the judge is going over the dog.

bitches are judged, the champions of both sexes and the winners dog and winners bitch (best of the class dogs and class bitches) will compete for best of breed. The judge will then select the Scottish Terrier that he feels represents the breed the best for that day.

This is the dog that will go into the Terrier Group for judging against the other Terrier best of breeds.

Again, there will be four placements in the Group and the first-place Terrier will go into the best in show competition. There will be seven dogs in this class, one for each Group. This judge will select the dog that he feels is the best dog in the show. Thus, a dog show that starts with 2,000 or 3,000 dogs will finish the day with one dog who has remained undefeated and goes best in show.

The judge is observing the line-up in the breed ring.

Down and back for the judge.

This is basically how a dog show functions. As a newcomer to showing a dog, you will want to work toward a championship for your dog. This may take only three months, but more likely it will take anywhere from six months to two years, depending upon how often you are able to attend shows and how well you can keep your dog in condition.

Rowland John's wrote in 1933: "What good judges cannot resist is a dog who, having a reasonable number of good points, is able to carry himself as if he owned the whole show." Holland Buckley wrote in 1913: "If the day goes against you, your selection of shows and judges is sufficiently large to

try again. The awards are, after all, only the expression of one man's judgment, and the best of them at times overlook virtues as well as they sometimes miss bad faults." Old advice but still good advice.

Remember, participating successfully in dog shows requires patience, perseverance, time, money, skill and talent. It is the only sport where the amateur and the professional compete on an equal footing. The average dog show competitor remains active for only four to five years. Personal commitments such as children, work, and other hobbies can be a problem to those who want to compete every weekend. More often, the competitor who does not win enough will find his interest in the sport waning. A poorly groomed dog, a poorly bred dog, a dog that does not like to show and a handler who will not take the time to learn how to handle well are all deterrents to staying with the sport of dog showing.

In the early years, dog showing was a sport of the wealthy who hired the professionals to handle and condition their dogs. An early exception was Howard Snethen of Shieling Kennel, who always conditioned and showed his dogs, capping his career with Best in Show at Westminster in 1945 with Ch. Shielings Signature. Even in this day, it is very difficult for an owner-handler to top all dogs at this show. Blanche Reeg of Blanart Kennels handled and conditioned her own dogs and had many top winners. Her Ch. Blanart Bewitching won the Lloyd Memorial trophy in 1959 and 1960 in addition to winning seven best in shows and numerous group placements.

Evelyn Kirk of Balachan Kennels decided that she could do as well as a professional handler and showed Ch. Balachan Night Hawk to four all-breed bests in show along with many group placements. Hawk was also the Lloyd Trophy winner for 1968. John Sheehan of Firebrand Kennels has bred, conditioned and shown ten different Scots to all-breed bests in show in both the United States and Canada, and his Ch. Firebrand's Bookmaker won 14 bests in show. Miriam Stamm and Cindy Cooke have piloted several dogs to the all-breed best in show spot in addition to being the only kennel in the breed which has won the Lloyd trophy seven times with six different dogs. In the early years, some of these dogs were

handled by Lena Kardos, but the later dogs were all shown and conditioned by either Miriam or Cindy.

All of these owner-handlers started the hard way. Evelyn Kirk wrote that when she showed Night Hawk, "I just held on the end of the leash tight." John Sheehan gave his dog a good bath with lots of shampoo and coat conditioner the night before his first show. Bob Bartos saw him in the ring and mentioned that he could help John with his fluffy dog if he was interested. Blanche Reeg showed for 15 years before she won a blue ribbon.

It took perseverance for all of these

Looking over the competition while working the dogs.

A big win for Ch. Hughcrest Bottoms Up—Best of breed from the Veterans class at the national specialty, Montgomery County 1985. Owner-handler, Christine Cook.

owner-handlers to reach the top spot at an all-breed show. They all have nightmare stories of their first year or two of showing. (And sometimes of the first dog they showed.) Many started with a handler, then decided to learn the handling skills themselves and along the way, there have been some fine professionals who have loved the breed and have helped these individuals.

In researching this project I ran across some writing I did for the *Bobtail Express* back in 1970 when I was still active in Old English Sheepdogs. Obviously, my days were numbered in the breed, as here's the ending of one of my last articles:

"Have you ever been in the ring with your 85-pound dog who is pulling your arm out of the socket while he's trying to lunge out of the gate that he can't see? After getting the situation under control and while flexing your fingers to see that the circulation is still in them, you look in the next ring where the Toy Poodles are scampering around and you think, "How nice it must be!" Several weeks ago I showed two Scottish Terriers at a match for a friend and found out just how nice it is. During the first class with a five-month-old male, I spent most of the time trying to find the little fellow and then wondered what to do with his tail . . . TAIL! By the time the ten-month-old female and I made the rounds, I learned that you have to get down to their level to work and consequently I finished

Above: The famous Ch. Carmichael's Fanfare, bred by Ruth C. Johnson, took best in show at Westminster in 1965, the pinnacle of achievements for an American show dog.

Below: Ch. Schwer's Dynamic Happy Boy, whelped 1970, bred by Wilfred and Mary Schwer, was a multi-best in show winner, including Montgomery County in 1973. Owners, Donald and Carol Plott.

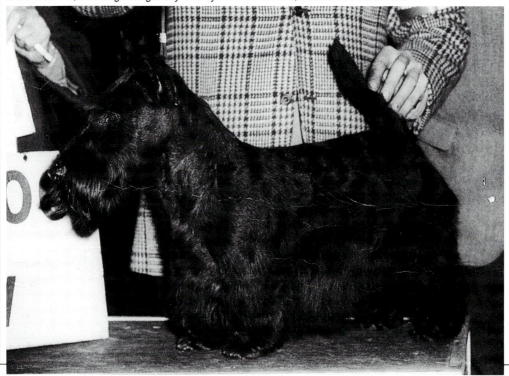

Westminster best in show winner 1985—Ch. Braeburn Close Encounter, bred by R.E. and H.M. Girling. Owners, Sonnie and Alan Novick.

that class with a couple of gaping holes around the region of the knee-caps. Since we had beginner's luck (breed and group one), I spent a considerable part of the day running around the ring on my knees. After I left the ring on our last run, I surveyed the ridges in my knees from the mats and my by now baggy, laddered panty hose. This was easy to do as I was having some difficulty in standing straight due to the pain in my back. When I arrived home I realized that I had also pulled every unused muscle in my legs and was having some difficulty in walking. However, throughout it all, my left arm remained in its socket and the dog did know where it was going every minute of the day and that was usually after the dog next to her! So, there are advantages and disadvantages to showing both small and large breeds."

I became more proficient in showing the Scottish Terriers and have always maintained that it takes strength to show a large breed and intelligence to show a small one.

Handler Bill Prentice with Ch. Barberrry Knowe Barbican at the 1951 Scottish Terrier Club of America show.

Professional Handlers

You should contact a professional handler if you want your dog shown and are unable to do it yourself. A professional handler is an individual whose livelihood is handling dogs, and often also boards and grooms dogs. Be sure to inquire about the background of a handler before handing your dog over. You will want a terrier handler and one who knows how to put a Scottish Terrier into a show coat. You will want a handler who wins. The handler should belong to the Professional Handlers Association (PHA) and he will be able to furnish one or two references if you feel this is neces-

sary. Be sure to inquire as to all costs and find out what will be expected from you as the owner of the dog. In return the handler will tell you what you can expect from him.

Through the years there have been professional handlers who have been true friends of the Scottish Terrier. These are individuals who have shown the great dogs and who have loved the breed. Most have been members of the STCA and have given freely of their time to help individuals within the breed and the regional breed clubs. Even though they have shown other breeds, their true love is the Scottie. Through their assistance with handling and their skills in grooming, many an owner-handler has been able to become a formidable competitor in the ring.

The Stalters of Barberry Knowe Kennels used the expertise of Bill Prentice when they began their kennel operation. John Marvin wrote that Bill Prentice was a Scotsman

Handler Johnny Murphy with Ch. Carmichael's Fanfare winning under breeder-judge Robert Graham at the STCA Specialty in 1963.

of great knowledge and good judgment. At one point Bill also was the handler and kennel manager for S.S. VanDine's Sporran Kennel. When Bill retired, his son Phil and daughter Florence were concurrently, or at different times, handler and kennel manager for Barberry Knowe. All three Prentices are now deceased.

Bob Bartos was kennel manager for Ted Bennett at Deephaven Kennels, and in 1947 he moved to Carnation Farms to manage their operation. An outstanding groomer and handler, he set high standards that handlers continue to try to follow to this day. He handled many imports and Carnation dogs to the best in show spot, but the high point was Best in Show at Westminster in 1967 with English and American Ch. Bardene Bingo. Bingo lived at home as a house dog with Bob and Jane until his death. John Sheehan from Firebrand made yearly trips to Carnation where Bob served as mentor, helping John with his grooming and advising him with his breeding program. Bob, an STCA member for many years, retired from Carnation and is presently an AKC-licensed judge.

Johnny Murphy came to the United States with the Scottish soccer team and never returned to live in his homeland. Greatly loved for his brogue and personality, he handled for the Barberry Knowe Kennel and the Marlu Kennel, in addition to handling for many other Scottie owners. The high point of his career was Best in Show at Westminster in 1965 with Ch. Carmichael's Fanfare. Johnny was instrumental in bringing together a group of Scottish Terrier owners who eventually formed the STC of Greater New York. He was always willing to give of his time to help a new exhibitor with handling or with grooming. Johnny retired from handling and became an AKC-licensed judge. His death in 1973 was a great loss to his many friends in the fancy.

Lena Kardos was an established West Coast terrier handler when she started

Handler Judy Hughes with Ch. Highcrest Jigger O' Gin winning best of winners at Montgomery County specialty under breeder-judge Bob Bartos.

Handler Lena Kardos (second from left) as a member of the first all-Scottie obedience and drill team in 1951.

handling Ch. Bardene Boy Blue for Tony and Miriam Stamm. The two teamed up to earn a best in show on their first outing. Lena continued to handle for the Stamms during their early years in dogs, showing Ch. Bardene Bobby Dazzler, who became the Lloyd Trophy winner in 1966. Lena handled a host of Scots to their championships and concluded her career with handling English import Ch. Gaywyn Likely Lad. Lena was well known on the West Coast, and many breeders sought out her advice. She has been an avid Scottie friend and was a member of the STCA for many years.

George Ward, another well-known terrier handler, achieved top wins with many terriers, but his legacy to the Scottish Terrier world is having shown Ch. Braeburn's Close Encounter to the top-winning dog of all time, all-breeds. In her years in the ring, "Shannon" became well known to exhibitors, spectators and judges, and brought many new friends to the breed. She was shown from 1980 through 1985 and her record included 371 bests of breed including including specialty bests of breed. She amassed 340 group firsts and 214 bests in show. She won 190 groups in a row and lost in the breed only four times. She was best in show at the prestigious shows of Kennel Club of Philadelphia (1983), Detroit Kennel Club (1984), Montgomery County Terrier Show (1984) and Chicago International (1985). In 1985 she was the sixth of the breed to win the Westminster Kennel Club show. She returned to the ring again as a veteran in 1990 and drew a large audience of spectators who were all anxious to once again see this great show girl make the rounds of the ring with George. She was shown, as usual, in superb condition, and the pair received an unusual show of respect as the audience stood and applauded. The breed has been fortunate to have had this exceptional dog and handler as goodwill ambassadors for our breed. Shannon spent her retirement years with George Ward and Roz Ward and died in 1994.

Tom Natalini of Stonehedge Kennel is a Scottish Terrier breeder and a professional handler. Tom is well known in the New York/New Jersey area for his personality, generosity and wit. He has given abundantly of his time to the breed, to the Scottish Terrier Club of Greater New York and to the Scottish Terrier Club of America. The author particularly appreciated his sharing many of the pictures for this book. It was of great sadness to the breed when his partner Don Massaker died suddenly in 1990.

Bergit Coady immigrated from Germany to the Reanda Kennel in England, then came to America and worked for Betty Malinka at the Sandoone Kennel. In the early 1970s, she moved to Southern California and has continued to be a top

Handler Tom Natalini with Ch. Kennelgarth Annabel winning under breeder-judge Richard Hensel. Annabel was owned by Stephen Specter and Peter Josten.

handler of terriers, with her particular love being the Scottish Terrier. She advised Dick Hensel of Dunbar Kennels with his breeding program and showed his Ch. Dunbar's Democrat of Sandoone to many bests in show. She handled all of Dick's dogs until his death. She has handled scores of Scots to their championship in addition to campaigning many of them to multiple group and best in show wins. She has given of her time to the STC of California and is well liked by her Scottie competitors as she is "always a lady." Bergit campaigned Louise Simon's Ch. Simonez Charlie the Charmer and Louise wrote about the wonderful job Bergit did with Charlie and she added "Best of all she loved him." Bergit is a member of the STCA.

Mark George, the youngest member of the group of handlers, will be remembered as a handler who has done much to advance the popularity of the wheaten Scottie. He has had phenomenal success with this color coat, which is not an easy coat to get into proper condition for the ring. The wheatens that he has handled have shown the public that this color can be presented in top condition with personalities to match their coat color. His winning wheatens have been numerous, but of particular note have been Ch. Sandgreg's Foxmoor and Ch. Sandgreg's Sweet Luv. Mark breeds Scotties in addition to showing them and has been a member of the STCA since his youth.

Above: Handler Mark George with Ch. Sandgreg's Desert Fox owned by Tony and Pat Gruda. Breeders, John and Barbara DeSaye.

Below: Handler Bergit Coady with Ch. Finn Varga Rex Coeur Illustre. Breeder-owner, Elaine Carrington.

Three generations of Firebrand Scottish Terrier bitches: **Top**: Ch. Firebrand's Pandora, by Am., Can. Ch. Firebrand's Bookmaker ex Ch. Viking's Camy Ann, whelped 1972, bred by John Sheehan and owned by the author.

Middle: Ch. Firebrand's Fair Weather, whelped 1976, by Scotsmuir Something Special ex Ch. Firebrand's Pandora, bred by the author.

Bottom: Ch. Firebrand's Winter Promise, whelped 1979, by Ch. Firebrand's Jack Knife ex Ch. Firebrand's Fair Weather, a group winner bred by the author.

Breeding Your Scottish Terrier

Several thoughts should be kept in mind when you consider breeding your Scottish Terrier.

1. Not every bitch needs to be bred. Take a look at your local humane society and see the numbers of unwanted dogs that will eventually be put down for lack of a home.

2. Do not breed your bitch because you want your children to see Mother Nature at work. There are good videos that can answer their questions.

3. Do not breed your bitch because you want to "make some money." It's just about impossible to make any money on a litter, and in general it will be a losing operation.

4. Do not breed your bitch because you think "one litter will be good for her." Is a woman "better" because she goes through childbirth?

Think about the following before having a litter of puppies:

1. A litter of puppies is very time consuming. You and the rest of the family will be spending hours with the puppies, cleaning them, worrying over them, socializing them.

2. A litter of puppies is very hard on the house. Rugs are not only soiled but they are often chewed around the corners, as well as the woodwork and furniture. Once outside, the pups can create havoc in the yard.

3. A litter of puppies will cost you money. First you have a stud fee. Then your bitch may require a Caesarian section, which is a substantial expense. Your puppies will require shots, a large expense if you have a large litter.

4. You cannot count on selling your puppies quickly. You may have one or two pups with you until six months of age or more. In the meantime, the family becomes attached to them, your dog food bills continue to rise and your patience runs thin.

If you do decide to breed, answer the following questions:

1. Is your bitch of quality? Does she have a good pedigree, linebred with a championship background? (And one champion out of 64 descendants does not make a championship background.)

2. Did you talk to the breeder that you bought your bitch from in regard to breeding her? Did she tell you that you should breed your girl or did she sell her to you as a pet?

3. What stud dog should you breed to? Ask your breeder for her opinion. Use a dog that has a solid pedigree, not only is he from a championship back-

155

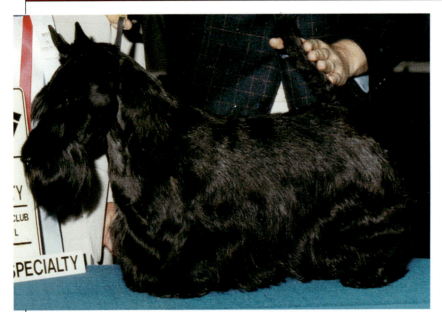

Eng., Am., Can. Ch. Scarista's Rocky, whelped 1983, by Int. Ch. Scarista Lord Snooty ex Millig Miss Marquessa, bred by James Falconer. Owners, Tom and Mary Parrotti. Rocky is a best in show winner and a prominent Scottie sire.

Rocky's son, Eng., Am., Can. Ch. Killisport Rox of Scarista, bred by Elizabeth M. Blower, was whelped in 1984. Jenny Wren of Scarista was the dam. Killisport was the top Scot in the United Kingdom. He won the breed at Crufts and Westminster and is a top producer. Owners, Tom Natalini, Irwin and Ilene Hochberg and Stonehedge Kennels.

ters are easier than fall and winter litters as you can have the puppies outside more. Do you have a big vacation planned for the summer? Is there already a glut of Scottie puppies in your area? Ask the reputable breeder, the one with the stud dog that is being used, and she can tell you.

A note in regard to the reputable, experienced breeders: These are individuals who have been breeding Scottish Terriers for ten to 20 or more years. They belong to an all-breed club and to the STCA. They show their dogs, attend the national shows and keep abreast of the trends in the breed. A wise new-

ground but he himself is a champion and possibly a group or best in show winner. The stud fee will not be much more than breeding to a mediocre dog.

4. When should you have this litter? Spring and summer lit-

comer will build upon their experience. Don't think that you can come along and breed a "star" with a pet shop bitch. This happens about as often as winning that lottery! Also remember, start with a quality bitch. You probably won't live long enough to breed up to the quality of the big winners of the day unless you start with quality.

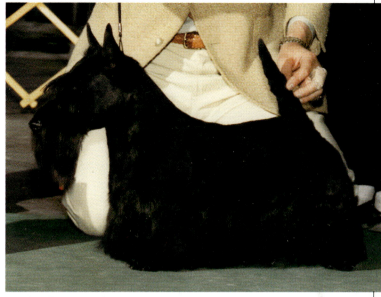

Another Rocky son, Ch. Killisport Charisma of Scarista, whelped 1985, bred by E. M. Blower, is a multi-group winner. Jenny Wren of Killisport was the dam. Owners, Bill and Kathy deVilleneuve.

You have decided that you have the quality dog that should be bred and you are going ahead with this project. You have talked to the breeder of your bitch and it's determined you should breed her. You have found a good stud dog and you are ready to get to work.

A Scottish Terrier bitch will come into season the first time when she is around eight to ten months old. She will come into season approximately every six months after that. Do not breed your bitch the first season. Wait until she is about eighteen months old and then consider breeding her.

You should contact the owner of the stud dog that you have selected when you first notice that your bitch is in season. You will be told when to bring her to the kennel so that she can be bred somewhere between the 11th and 15th days of her estrus.

Your girl has now been bred and by the sixth week of gestation (gestation for dogs is 63 days), you should know if she is pregnant. Decide which room will be the nursery, making sure that you have picked a quiet spot out of the hubbub of daily living. Sometimes you can borrow a whelping box from another breeder, otherwise a box can be easily made. Scotties have a tendency to chew up cardboard cartons, thus a wooden box is better. A 3' by 3' pen is sufficient and the sides should be about 8 to 12 inches high. A guard rail (also called a "pig rail") should be placed around the inside of the box, approximately three inches above the ground. This gives the puppies an area to crawl under for protection against the mother's weight when she leans against the side of the box.

Start taking the bitch's temperature with a rectal thermometer about the 59th day after the first breeding. A dog's temperature averages about 101.5 degrees and as the whelping become more imminent the temperature will start to drop. When it settles down to 98 degrees or so you should be expecting pups within 24 hours. During these days you will also note a sticky and smelly discharge from the vulva and by now your girl should be quite heavy and may need assistance with the steps. Hold her on your lap and you can feel the puppies moving around!

Scottish Terrier litters average between three and six in a litter. Puppies will usually be delivered anywhere from 20-minute to three-hour intervals. It's a good idea when the first puppy is delivered to note the time of day, sex and color of the puppy on a note pad. If you should have a long delay between births, you will have specific information to give your veterinarian if you need to call for assistance.

Puppies are born in a sac and they are attached to the sac by the umbilical cord. Do not break this sac as the pup is emerging from the birth canal. Have patience as it can take up to ten minutes before the pup in the sac "pops" out. When the pup comes out, mother should reach around, open the sac and snip off the umbilical cord with her teeth. She will then wash up the pup. She may seem rough to you but she wants to stimulate the puppy and clear its lungs. Keep in mind that you may have to open the sac, cut the umbilical cord with blunt scissors and rub the puppy down with a towel. What you want to hear, whether you or the mother is doing the work, is a good, lusty cry from the pup.

Puppies and bitch should be kept in a draft-free, warm area. Take the mother outside after the whelping is completed and let her relieve herself. Clean up her rear end, put down clean towels or rugs in your box, and make her a dish of soft food. Give this to her along with a pan of water.

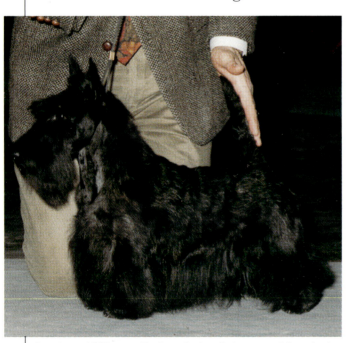

Daughter of Killisport, Ch. Stonehedge Galaxy out of Stonehedge Daisy Mae won the breed over specials at 11 months of age. Owners, Don Massaker, Tom Natalini, and Barbara Snobel.

Above: *Ch. Kellscots Rockslide CG, whelped 1988, bred by Lynn and John Kelley, by Eng., Am., Can. Ch. Scarista's Rocky ex Ch. Kellscots Pacesetter. Owner, Lynn Huffaker.*

Below: *Ch. Suzanne of Scarista, whelped 1985, by Ch. Killisport Rox of Scarista ex Linchow Alexis. Breeders, Mrs. M. McKeller. Owners, Irwin and Ilene Hockberg.*

RAISING A HEALTHY LITTER

Your litter has now been whelped. The first five days of your puppies' lives are their most important ones.

You can do some simple things to help ensure healthy puppies: keep the whelping box and the puppies in a draft-free area; keep the temperature in the whelping room at a minimum of 75 degrees; see that your mother is staying healthy, eating well, and drinking water.

This is what you want to see when you look in your whelping box: A contented mother and a contented litter. Your mother should be eating well, drinking water and giving off an air of well-being. The puppies should be tucked up around her, alternately sleeping and nursing. They should be quiet, happy and warm.

A newborn Scot by Ch. Anstamm Venture ex Wayridge Dark Gypsy. Breeders, Donald and Carol Plott.

Watch for the following trouble signs: Body temperature drop, no weight gain, dehydration. Check for dehydration by pinching the skin.

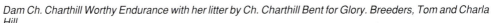

Dam Ch. Charthill Worthy Endurance with her litter by Ch. Charthill Bent for Glory. Breeders, Tom and Charla Hill.

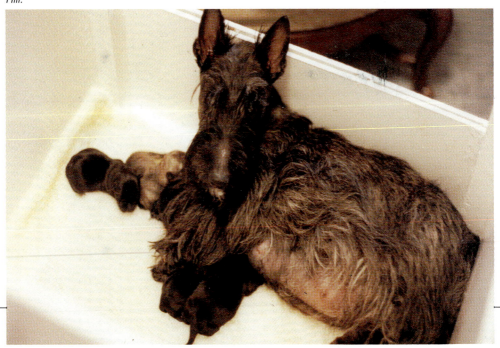

On a healthy pup, the skin pops back into place. On a dehydrated pup, the skin stays pinched. If your mother appears listless or if your whole litter starts crying, you have a problem. Call your veterinarian and tell him that you are bringing your bitch in, and ask him if he also wants to see the puppies.

Scottie puppies a few days old will look like little Labrador puppies.

Remember this when raising a litter: most litters are healthy litters. Your puppies will usually survive and your mothers will usually be attentive and healthy.

You should do whatever you can to ensure that the above takes place. Keep your whelping pen clean—an easy job for the first two weeks or so as mother does most of the work.

Feed your mother properly. If it is a large litter, you will probably have to increase her food, feeding her several times a day when the pups are approximately three weeks old. Look each puppy over every day and make sure that everything is functioning.

A short aside about dying pups: pups do die, no matter how you might try to save them. Here is a general rule of thumb: a cold puppy is a dead puppy. A puppy that the mother persistently ignores and pushes to the side of the pen will usually be a dead puppy within a matter of hours. Something is wrong with the pup, and mother knows it. Use your discretion about how much you want to do to save this kind of puppy.

Let's assume that all

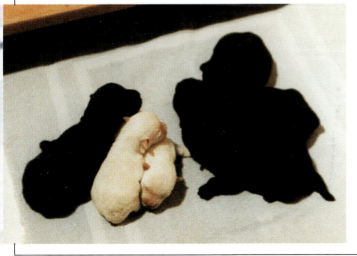

A litter of blacks and wheatens beginning to sleep in rows.

A pile of Scots from Deblin.

but it is not unusual for a Scottie to wait for 16 or 18 days. Many breeds are up on their legs at ten days. Again, Scotties are in no hurry and will not be very active until close to four weeks—and they will be unsteady until five weeks or so.

Start weaning your litter at three to four weeks. The larger the litter, the

is going well and that your litter is bobbing along, getting fat and keeping happy. Remember that our breed, with their short legs, is generally slow in developing. Many breeds open their eyes at ten days

more important it is to start weaning early to help mother with the feeding.

When you start to wean your puppies, mix up a gruel of puppy chow and a small portion of an all-

A one-and-a-half-week-old litter at Charthill.

162

Above: A cute young pup—ears up and ready to go!

Below: Wheatens are wheaten from birth. Breeder, Ruth Ann Krause.

meat dog product. Make a very mushy meal with no lumps in it. Serve it to the puppies in a very shallow pan. Cake pans work well. Remember, our breed has short legs and they have difficulty reaching into pans with high sides. At the time you start to feed your pups, offer them a pan of water also. As the pups start to eat more on their own and as their teeth start to come in, the mother will become less and less interested in spending time with the pups.

When your puppies are five to six weeks old, take them to your veterinarian for their shots. Your vet will tell you which shots they should have and how many times

Brother and sister at eight weeks before their first grooming.

Eight-week-old wheaten Scots after their first grooming. Breeder, Ruth Ann Krause.

they need to be repeated. At this time, you should take in a stool sample for analysis. If your pups are wormy, your veterinarian will give you the proper medication to clear up the worms.

By the time your pups are six weeks old, you will want to start some grooming. You should have already trimmed the toenails several times, but now it is time to "get serious."

Trim the head with your clippers so that you can see what you have. Trim the ears. The more hair you take off the ears at an early age, the quicker the ears will go up. Trim around the feet with scissors and be sure to trim the fanny and the tail. Now, you have little adult Scotties.

Most breeders like to keep their pups until they are about 12 weeks old—since they are so slow in maturing. However, if you have a potential buyer who has had a dog for ten or 12 years and is ready for a young one, you may consider selling the puppy at an earlier age.

When the pup goes to its new home,

A growing Scot from Stonehedge Kennel.

have it cleaned and trimmed up to look like a Scottie. Give the new owner a list of the food that you've been using and note the number of times a day that you are feeding. Give him the name of a veterinarian in his area. It's nice to add one of the little Scottie breed books and a leash, too. Of course, send the registration papers and a copy of the pedigree.

With your first litter, it may be hard to see the rascals go off to a new home. However, keep in mind that it is rather nice to have one of these little bundles that you have spent so much time on, go off into its own little world and be appreciated and loved.

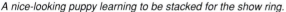
A nice-looking puppy learning to be stacked for the show ring.

A three-month-old litter at Ayr Scotties out of Lochlan's Rockette Max of Ayr.

The six-week-old "Rosie"—later to be Ch. Charthill Tiger Rose.

Olive as a puppy—later became Ch. Kellscots Pacesetter. Owner, Lynn Huffaker.

Looking alert.

A Stonehedge puppy.

Above Left: *Ch. Viewpark Heatherbelle, whelped 1974, by Aberscot Acquisition of Viewpark ex Viewpark Mayfair. Breeder, A.N. MacLaren. Owner, Lee Hastings.* **Above Right:** *Am., Can. Ch. Barraglen's Ballad, whelped 1973, by Ch. Gosmore Eilburn Admiration ex Woodhart Whimsical. Breeder-owners, Alan & Ann Bower.*

Below Left: *Ch. Hillview's Friar Tuck, whelped 1979, by Ch. Firebrand's Jack Knife ex Hillview's Anastasia. Breeder, Janet Bartholomew. Owner, John Sheehan.* **Below Right:** *Ch. Sparwyn Speak N' Spar, whelped 1989, by Ch. Sparwyn Chip Off the Old Block ex Am., Can. Ch. Hughcrest Strut N' Spar. Breeders, Deborah Mackie & Judy Hughes. Owner, Deborah Mackie.*

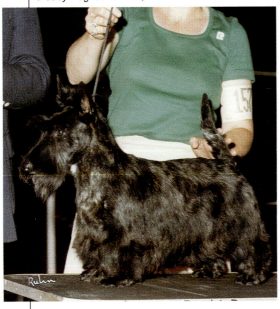

Above: Ch. Simonsez Charlie the Charmer, whelped 1982 by Ch. Enchanter of Eilburn ex Ch. Pack Run Marimax. Breeder-owner, E. Louise Simon.

Below: Am., Can. Ch. Starbelle Diamond Lil, whelped 1989, by Ch. Rosha's Bristol Cream ex Sanden Amber Belle Star. Breeder-owner, Damaris Batch.

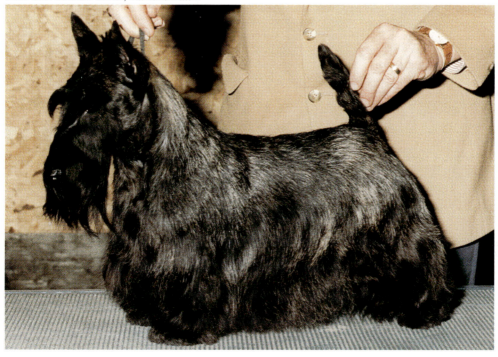

Above: *Am., Can. Ch. McVan's Ebony Rose, whelped 1986, by Am., Can. Ch. Glenecker's Galivanter ex Am., Can. Ch. Maggie McMuffin V. Breeder-owner, Dr. Vandra Huber.*

Below: *Ch. Kellscots Headstart, whelped 1984, by Ch. McArthur's CC of Maranscot. Breeders, Lynn & John Kelley. Owners, Joseph & Jean Huffaker & Lynn Huffaker.*

Above Left: *Ch. Firebrand's Ringmaster, whelped 1987, by Ch. Reanda Royal Soverign ex Ch. Firebrand's Viking Duchess. Breeder-owner, John Sheehan.* **Above Right:** *Ch. Ramtree Stonehedge KG Arthur, by Ch. Stonehedge Bandmaster ex Ch. Marlorain Lolita. Owners, Marlorain Kennels.*

Below Left: *Ch. Deblin's Back Talk, whelped 1984, by Ch. Anstamm All American ex Ch. Deblin's Small Talk. Breeders, Deborah Brookes & Lynn Struck.* **Below Right:** *Ch. Uncanny's Go Your Own Way, whelped 1984, by Ch. Aerie Deal with the Laidies ex Ch. Uncanny's A Little Night Music. Breeder-owners, Jane S. & John Anderson.*

Left: Ch. MacPooch Ms Michie, whelped 1983, by Ch. Schaeffer's Calling Card ex Ch. Amescot Miss Christie. Breeders, Mr & Mrs. Rubenstein. Owners, Luis Arroyo & Thomas Callahan. Handler, Ron Schaeffer.

Right: Am., Can. Ch. Lochnel Sae Sonsie O'Charlain, whelped 1985, by Ch. Sandgreg's Editorial ex Ch. Terriwall's Fire 'N Ice. Breeders, Andrew S. Boatwright & Charlene Hallenbeck. Shown with owner-handler Andrew Boatwright a top-winning junior handler.

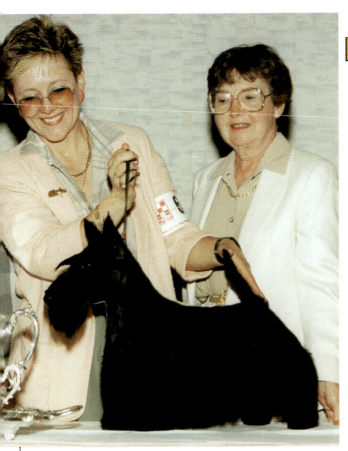

Left: Ch. Anstamm Heat Wave, whelped 1987, by Ch. Anstamm Summer Lightning ex Gayla's Mercedes Venture. Breeder, Gayla Schaubel. Owner-handler, Cindy Cooke and owner, Miriam Stamm.

Right: Ch. Charthill Tiger Rose, whelped 1989, by Ch. Charthill Worthy of Colwick ex Ch. Charthill Bridget by Briggs. Breeders, Charla Hill & Susan Ilfring. Owners, Tom & Charla Hill. Handled by Charla Hill.

Left: *Ch. Duff-De Pac Man, whelped 1982, by Ch. Wychwood Beau Geste ex Duff-De Tootsie Roll. Breeder-owners, Bill & Kathy deVilleneuve. Trophy presenter, Jackie Seelbach, STCA president.*

Right: *Ch. Jabberwok Here Comes The Sun, whelped 1981, with owner-handler, Merle Taylor, winning best of breed at Montgomery County national specialty show 1983 under breeder-judge Howard Sneethan.*

Right: Ch. Vikland's Curtain Call. Breeder-owner and handler, Kathy Bowers.

Left: Ch. Wychwood Beau Geste, whelped 1979, by Ch. Schaeffer's Marco Polo ex Ch. Am Anger Glendale Star. Owner-handler, Jean C. Ferris.

Above: Eng., Am. Ch. Woodmansey Wait For It, whelped 1979, by Eng. Ch. Woodmansey Watchdog ex Woodmansey Whimsical. Owner-handler, Antonella Visconti Di Modrone with judge Robert Graham.
Below: Ch. Sandgreg's Annie Get Your Gun, whelped 1990, by Ch. Glengloamin's Berkley Square ex Ch. Sandgreg's Sweet Scarlet. Breeders, John & Barbara DeSaye. Owners, Joseph Pendon & Barbara DeSaye.

Above: *Ch. Koch's Rambo Of Aberglen, by Ch. Sandgreg's Foxmoor ex Ch. Glad Mac's Georgette. Breeder, John DeSaye. Handler, Rick Fowler. Owners, Debby Fowler, Jan Beaman & Mark George.*

Below: *Ch. Glenby Gallant Ruler, by Ch. Glenby Gallant Lad. Breeder-owners, Fred & Christine Stephens. Shown winning under Breeder-judge, Elizabeth Cooper. Handled by Owner Christine Stephens.*

Above: *Ch. Kellscots Pacesetter, whelped 1985, by Ch. McArthur's Constant Challenge ex McArthur's CC of Maranscot. Owner-handler, Lynn Huffacker Judge, Muriel Lee. Breeders, Lynn & John Kelley.*
Below: *Ch. Starr's Boulder Legend, whelped 1989, by Ch. Boulder Legend Landslide ex Paroba's Lady Bridgett. Breeder-judge, Tom Kirk. Handler, Lisalott Johansson. Owner, Robin Starr. Breeder, Virginia Paroba.*

179

Above: Ch. Stonehedge Thunderbolt. Breeders, Tom Natalia & Don Massaker & John & Alice Gomes. Handler, Don Massaker.

Below: Ch. Charthill Seaworthy, whelped 1989, by Ch. Charthill Worthy of Colwick ex Ch. Charthill Colwick Courtney. Handler, Tom Hill . Judge, Alice Watkins and trophy presenter, Betty McArthur.

Below: Ch. Firebrand's Sunday Scherzo, whelped 1981, by Ch. Firebrand's Paymaster ex Firebrand's Thursday Musical. Breeder, Muriel Lee. Owners, John Sheehan & Dayton & Jean Thornton.

Above: Ch. Gaelforce Post Script by Ch. Glad Mac's Tailliesin The Bard ex Ch. Glenlee's Sable Fox. Owner, Vandra L. Huber. Post Script won Best of Breed at Montgomery County national specialty in 1993.

Below: Ch. Sandgreg's Second Edition with three of his get, winning the stud dog class at national specialty, Montgomery County 1988. Handled by John DeSaye.

181

Above: *Ch. Bar-Nones' Troubles Brewin, whelped 1983, by Ch. Hughcrest Home Brew ex Ch. Hughcrest Bottoms Up. Breeder-owner-handler, Christine Cook & Breeder-judge, Bill Justus.*

Below: *Ch. Hughcrest Bottoms Up, whelped 1977, by Ch. Dunbar's Democrat of Sandoone ex Ch. Hughcrest Happy Hour. Owners, C. Michael & Christine Cook. Handler, Christine Cook.*

A charming moment with Ch. Gaelforce Post Script, a best in show Scottie who has placed in the group over 50 times and went best of breed at Westminster 1994 under judge Barbara Keenan. Owner, Vandra L. Huber. Photo by Holloway.

183

The Scottish Terrier loves the great outdoors as much as the next big dog.

Some Scots love water... whether a garden hose or a garden pond.

Health

By and large, the Scottish Terrier is considered to be a healthy breed, relatively free from genetic problems and often known for longevity.

William Haynes wrote in 1925: "The terrier owner is a 'lucky devil' for his dogs do not, as a rule, spend a great deal of time in the hospital. All members of the terrier family, from the giant of the race, the Airedale, way down to little Scottie, owe a big debt to Nature for having blessed them with remarkably robust constitutions. Even when really sick, they make wonderfully rapid recoveries. It is almost a joke to keep such a naturally healthy dog as a terrier in the pink of condition. All he needs is dry, clean kennels with decent bedding; good, nourishing food at regular hours; all the fresh water he wants to drink; plenty of exercise, and a little grooming. Given these few things and a terrier will be disgustingly well, full of high spirits, and happy as a clam at high tide."

As Mr. Haynes wrote, a Scottie is normally a thrifty dog. Give him care, use your commonsense and have a good veterinarian available. Find a reliable veterinarian that you trust, take your dog in when you think that you have a problem, follow instructions and recovery will usually be very rapid. Your dog should have yearly inoculations along with having a stool sample run to make certain that he is free from worms. Keep the teeth clean and the nails trimmed. Your veterinarian can do these jobs if you or your groomer are unable to do so. Watch for ticks in the summer, and any wounds should be cleaned out. Some of them may require veterinary care. Yearly heartworm checks in some areas of the country are also important.

If your veterinarian is not available at odd hours for emergencies, know where the emergency veterinarian is located and keep his telephone number handy. Many veterinarians in large cities no longer have an emergency service and you must rely on these special facilities for late evening, weekend and holiday services.

Keep your dog groomed and clean. Keep him out of the sun in the summer and certainly don't leave him in the car during a hot day. The dark coats can soak up sun and heat and the two combined can cause severe heat problems for any dog.

Watch your Scot around the water. They are not good swimmers, probably due to the short legs. Many have drowned in swimming pools, unable to stay afloat or to climb out.

Your dog should be kept in either a fenced yard or on a leash. It's foolish and often against the law to let your dog run loose and take a chance of being run over by a car.

Too often the story is heard about the dog that lives at the end of the cul-de-sac where only one delivery truck comes a day, and that truck runs over the dog. It only takes one vehicle to shorten a dog's life.

Dogs often live to seven or eight years and then die of some disease. It seems that if your Scot lives to eight years of age, your chances are good that you will have another two to six years with him. Eleven- and twelve-year-old Scotties are not unusual. Remember anything after eight years, in any breed, is usually a gift.

A few particular Scottie problems should be mentioned. They are: Scottie cramp, von Willebrand's disease, epileptic seizures and cancer.

Scottie cramp is an inherited neurological disorder that is seen only in the Scottish Terrier. Studies are still being undertaken but it appears to be carried by a recessive gene. It can show up in a pup as early as six to eight weeks of age, but more likely it will manifest at about six months. The Scottie will be running and playing hard and the rear legs will start to stiffen up (cramp). The body then becomes drawn up and arched, the forelegs stiffen and the dog falls over. In a few seconds, he recovers and is back on his feet. Dogs affected by Scottie cramp can be wonderful pets and their condition can be reduced by giving affected dogs vitamin E or diazepam, both given on a daily basis. Dogs exhibiting any degree of Scottie cramp should not be bred.

Von Willebrand's disease (VWD) is the most common mild bleeding disorder of man and dogs and affects many breeds. This is an inherited disease carried by a recessive gene. Scotties can either be free of VWD, be carriers of the gene, or be "bleeders." Reputable breeders have their animal's blood tested to make sure

Scots wading around.

that they are not breeding dogs who carry or have VWD. Dogs who score 60 and above on their blood test are considered to test normal for VWD. Those who score in the 50 to 59 range are borderline normal and should be bred only to dogs with a normal score. Care should be taken in breeding those who score below 50 and certainly if the

Alert and healthy Scots.

dog is bred, it should be bred to a dog that scores in the normal range for VWD.

Epileptic seizures, convulsions and "fits" are terms used to describe the same event: recurrent seizures caused by a disturbance of brain function. The seizure occurs suddenly and lasts about one minute, and the dog recovers spontaneously. The dog loses consciousness, his limbs and trunk stiffen and he falls over on his side with severe rigidity of the muscles alternating with vigorous running motions. This will be usually accompanied by biting motions and salivation.

Recovery is complete but sometimes there may be a period of disorientation before complete recovery. There are variations to seizures but most owners will realize that their dog is having a seizure by the second occurrence.

At this time, the cause of seizures, the reasons for them, and who will have a seizure are still being studied. If you feel your dog is subject to seizures, you should take him to the veterinarian; he will prescribe an anticonvulsant drug and the condition will be kept under control. Seizures are a common problem in dogs and many can live a normal life with the anticonvulsant drug. There is no evidence that seizures are painful to a dog and often the owner is much more upset in watching the disturbing event than is the dog, who is unaware of what is happening.

Cancer diagnosis can happen in any breed of dog and Scotties are no exception. As in man, there is not always a cure and again as in man, early detection is your best form of prevention. Check your dog over each time you groom him for any lumps or bumps that you have not noticed before. Fast-growing lumps are cause for concern, particularly when found around the mammary glands. Any lump that you do not like the look of or is growing rapidly should be checked by your veterinarian.

THE GERIATRIC DOG

The geriatric dog, a dog over eight years of age, may require a little more or different care than the younger dog. As your dog ages, he will slow down and possibly have some arthritis. His sight and hearing start waning and he may sleep more. Let him have his way. Do not expect him to do the three-mile walk as he did as a pup. You may want to try dog food for the geriatric or sedate dog. Be sure he has a warm space to sleep and try to keep him at a normal weight, as excess weight can be difficult on the rheumatoid bones.

As he ages and becomes more infirm, you will eventually be confronted with the decision of putting your dog down. Unfortunately, dogs and humans do not die very often in their sleep. With the dog, though,

Some Scots are homebodies and some are quite adventurous, always seeking to explore new territory.

Half the battle is a healthy outlook on the world.

we are able to make the decision to be a humane owner and the day may come when you take your pet in to be euthanized by your veterinarian. It's hard to know when "it's time" but again use your commonsense and try not to let the dog suffer unduly. Your veterinarian will administer a very quick drug and you will be surprised as to how quickly and peacefully he will die in your arms. This is a terribly sad day for the entire family, but it often takes only a few weeks or months before you are off looking for your new Scottish Terrier.

189

A Scottie who's proven an all-around winner—MacKeever UD, ILP, whelped 1982, was a rescue dog and went on to finish the highest of all AKC obedience titles. Owner-handler, Louise De Blois.

Working with a Scottish Terrier

Every Scottish Terrier should be able to lay around the house, have a good meal, receive love and attention and be taken for a walk or a romp every day. However, some owners like the challenge of working with their dog, of training him to follow commands and of seeing him performing the chores that he was bred to do. With terriers, an owner can work in obedience, train in agility or send his dog to ground in a working trial. It is surely challenging to work a Scot but it can be done, and an owner can have a tremendous feeling of accomplishment once a goal is set and reached.

OBEDIENCE

Scotties are not an easy breed to work with in obedience. With their intelligence and independent spirit, they can sometimes be more trying to train than had been anticipated. You will see Golden Retrievers, Poodles and Miniature Schnauzers in abundance in obedience classes as these are breeds which are easy to work with; they are intelligent, but more importantly, they have a willingness to please their master. Scotties don't always want to please and they can quickly become bored with working the same exercise over and over again.

In spite of these difficulties, Scotties do complete obedience degrees and some individuals have been very successful with training them up to the highest degree of work, the Utility degree. For obedience work, dog and handler need aptitude and determination. The handler must take time to work his dog every day, even if it is only for five minutes or so. The handler must also have patience, and the dog must have a desire to perform and at least some willingness to please. Once this match is made, a handler and his dog can be well on their way toward obedience degrees.

Munro's Dark Chunk O' Chocolate clearing the high jump.

The handler will feel a tremendous amount of achievement and accomplishment to have such a smart little dog working by his side. Spectators at a dog show love to watch the obedience rings, as they can understand what the dog is doing (or not doing) much better than when they watch the conformation rings. There is no better sight than watching the Scot, with his short legs, flying over the hurdles.

Obedience classes are offered throughout the country, and unless you live in a very remote area, your town or city should offer you a selection of training clubs. Some classes are offered by private individuals, others by obedience clubs or all-breed clubs. There are different methods of instruction, and you may find it worthwhile to visit various classes to see which method of training you prefer.

You will usually start your pup at about six months of age; some classes will not take a dog any younger. Classes will meet once or twice a week for six to ten weeks. Having successfully completed one of these classes, and successful means passing the examination at the end of the class, you should have a dog that will sit on command, come when called and walk decently on a lead. This is all that many dog owners require. They want a pet that behaves like a gentleman or a lady. If you have never owned a dog before, or never owned a dog with good manners, obedience class work may be just what you want and need.

Obedience trials take practice. "Casey" is working on the high jump with the dumbbell.

"Casey" practicing the broad jump.

For those who have a genuine interest in obedience, your class work will continue beyond this and you will start working for degrees and titles, just as you would with a dog in the conformation ring. At this point, if you have not been training with an obedience club you may want to consider finding one that you can join.

"Casey" practicing the long stay.

193

The American Kennel Club offers the following obedience titles: Companion Dog (CD) is earned in Novice class, Companion Dog Excellent (CDX) is earned in Open class and a Utility Dog (UD) degree and a Utility Dog Excellent (UDX) are earned in the Utility class and beyond.

To earn a degree, the dog must qualify for at least 170 of the 200 points at a trial. When a dog has qualified, he has earned a "leg" and three legs under three different judges must be earned before the dog receives his title. Once

Ashmoor Maggie Munroe CD, on the Novice recall exercise.

Reed's Highland Heather UD, on the broad jump.

a title is earned, it becomes a part of the dog's name, just as Ch. (Champion) becomes a part of the name when won in the conformation ring. Obedience titles are added at the end of the name rather than at the beginning.

In an obedience trial you are competing against yourself. If there are 20 in the class and ten receive scores of 170 or more, ten dogs will receive their leg at that show. In conformation showing you compete against all other dogs as there is only one best of breed dog.

Novice classes consist of heeling on lead, standing for examination, coming when called and the long sit (one minute) and the long down (three minutes). In Open classes, all work is done off lead, which includes heeling, coming when called, dropping to a down position on command, retrieving a dumbbell and jumping over the broad jump. In Utility the exercises become much more complicated and include hand signals, scent exercises and directed jumping. As can be seen, these are ambitious programs requiring great effort and patience on both the handler's and the dog's part.

If you decide to work toward an obedience degree, lessons and class work are just about essential. Daily practice is also a must. If you become active in an obedience club, you will be aware of the obedience matches that are offered in your area. A match is an opportunity for you to work your dog in a show-like setting without paying the fee required for entering a licensed AKC obedience trial. Entry fees for a match are minimal and judging will be done by amateurs who have done extensive obedience work. You cannot earn any "legs" at a match, but you will learn how a show works and what will be required of you and your dog.

Scottish Terriers have been active in obedience work for decades. The first Scottie to earn his obedience title was a son of Ch. Heather Goldfinder, earning his CD in 1938. Mrs. Bertha Russell finished two obedience champions in the 1940s:

Ch. Glenby Miss Andrea CDX was one of two Scots to gain obedience titles in the 1940s. Owner-handled by Bertha Russell, she earned CD, CDX and conformation championship between May and November 1946.

Ch. Glenby Bonnie CD and Ch. Glenby Miss Andrea CDX. Dorissa Barnes, who wrote the first obedience article in a STCA Handbook (1972), wrote of being a member of a drill team of six Scots who performed for the Scottish Terrier Club of California. Ms. Barnes's bitch was seven years old when she started obedience work, which shows that obedience can be started at any age. A Scottie named Eliza Doolittle, owned by Diane Williams of Tennessee, earned all of her obedience titles plus a Tracking Dog title, work that is ordinarily performed by hunting and working dogs.

The STCA offers several annual trophies for obedience work in addition to offering pewter medallions to all who complete an obedience title. In the late 1980s, the STCA started offering match shows in conjunction with the national specialty weekend in Pennsylvania.

STCA members who have worked actively with their dogs and have given unstintingly of their time to promote the sport of obedience in the Scottie world are Bert and Ruth Tryon, Letty Passig, Faith Harrup and Lorraine Lapin.

One exceptional winning Scottie in obedience was the Tryons' Ch. Milady Vivacious Agnes CDX who was high in trial, which is the equivalent of winning best in show at a conformation show . . . a great achievement for any dog but particularly for the hard-to-train Scot. Sharon Flodin-Specktor's bitch, Firebrand's Just Right, achieved the titles of CD, CDX and UD. Of her offspring, Gleannloch's Raffle Ticket, owned by Peggy Gerold, earned his UD (the second Scot that Peggy has put a UD on) and two other of her offspring have completed their CDXs.

The most heartwarming of the obedience stories is the tale of MacKeever (sire and dam unknown) owned by Louise DeBlois of New Jersey. MacKeever was a rescue dog, having come from a pet shop where he was scheduled to be put down as no one had wanted to give him a home. Louise's husband visited the pet shop often, befriended MacKeever, and eventually brought him home to join the household of two aged Irish Setters. Louise had trained an Irish Setter and a German Shorthaired Pointer to Utility degrees and put her hand to work with MacKeever. He completed his CD in three shows with scores in the 190s, his CDX in five shows and his UD with scores in the 180s. He is now ten years old and still comes out for a veterans class on occasion. Louise noted that she has become a fan of the breed for life. That's a story for you! A rescue tale, an obedience saga and a love story. Lucky dog—lucky owner.

AGILITY TRIALS

Agility is a relatively new sport having come to the United States from England. The handler and the dog, working as a team, go through a timed obstacle course. Scoring is simple and objective, based upon the dog's completing all of the obstacles and the speed with which this is accomplished.

In order to compete in this sport, you must belong to an all-breed club or an obedience club where there are

Hiwood Scarlett of Munro clearing the rail hurdle at an agility trial.

Top: Ayrlawn Egar Alen Po of Hiwood negotiating the A-frame.

Middle: Ch. Ayrlawn Robert the Bruce crossing the dog walk.

Bottom: Ch. Ayrlawn Henry VII of Hiwood heading for the open tunnel.

Going to ground in California.

Miss Bonnyfied Busy Bee CD, TD, CG going to ground. Handler, Lynn Huffaker.

Three terrific obedience Scots: Miss Bonnyfied Busy Bee CD, TD, CG, McArthur's CC of Maranscot CG and Ch. McArthur's Constant Challenge CG. Handler, Lynn Haffaker.

individuals who support this event. The obstacle course requires substantial space and the obstacles themselves are fairly extensive.

Basic obstacles are a see-saw, pipe tunnel, collapsed tunnel and some weave poles. Jumps and hurdles will include the broad jump, tire jump, and high jump. Jumps are equal to at least the dog's height at the withers and never more than one-and-a-half times the height.

Many dog shows now hold agility as an exhibition. The ring is easy to find as spectators can be four deep around the entire area. A great deal of enthusiasm emanates from all quarters: cheers from the spectators, barking from the dogs and loud encouragement from the handlers. This is a fun sport and not for the weak of heart!

WORKING TRIALS

Scottish Terriers are bred to go to ground after vermin and small rodents. Even if most Scots have not been required to use these skills on an everyday basis, the instinct remains in a well-bred Scot. Everyone is familiar with the rapt attention a Scottie will give a squirrel that

Top: Miss Bonnyfied Busy Bee CD, TD, CG, on a TDX track with Lynn Huffaker.

Middle: Ch Munro's Dark Squire Brown about to enter the tunnel.

Bottom: Scot going to ground.

Top: Oak Brourne's Rowdy McGruff is a police-trained Scottish Terrier owned by Janet Noble of Freedom, California. McGruff does building searches, area and article searches in addition to narcotics work. Janet was a police officer and had trained her German Shepherd when McGruff was added to her household; she included him in the training. Janet wrote: "He does bite work but is so sound in his temperament that he participated in a multitude of K-9 demonstrations with pre-school and handicapped children. He was great to start the demonstrations with as he did not intimidate the children as the Shepherd could. He "warmed up the audience, so to speak!"

Right: Jeanni Pasmore's trick Scottie entertains in nursing homes.

crosses his path, the quickness to find a mouse in the kennel, or the speed with which he can flush out a rabbit in a field. The short-legged terriers were used to drag the prey out of their dens or to force the vermin to bolt from their dens. On occasion, they would hold the prey at bay to indicate the location for their master.

The American Working Terrier Association offers Certificates of Gameness at sanctioned trials. The STCA recognizes certificates from the club and from the Potomac Cairn Terrier Club. Scots are put through the requirements beginning in the Novice class. The dog must enter a ten-foot-long tunnel buried in the ground, which will include one right-angle turn. He can take any amount of time to enter the tunnel, but he must reach the prey in one minute and then work the prey for 30 seconds. If he completes these tasks in the required time, with no encouragement other than the command given when he is released to enter the tunnel, he will have qualified in the Novice class, and then moves up to the Open class.

In the Open class, the tunnel is 30 feet long with a minimum of three right-angle turns. He again must reach the prey in 30 seconds and work the prey for one minute without stopping.

Working trials, like obedience trials, are open to dogs of all ages. Again, the sport requires a willingness to compete on the Scot's part and the usual patience and perseverance on the owner's part.

I have also known of a Scot who was not trained in any of the above activities but who, along with his huntsman owner, participated in many a hunting trip in Northern Minnesota and Canada. He was active in moose, goose and duck hunting as well as in the fishing boat. His first time out, however, he fell off the dock into the water and, as they watched him bob up and down, the Indian guide pointed and said "Drowning, can't swim," and the owner quickly realized that Scots are not a water breed.

SANDY

Small head, but with brain enough for two,
Sandy's the dog that will see you through,
On the trail, sturdy, and stern, and dour,
As the wind that sweeps a Scottish moor.
In at the death, aye, Sandy's all there,
Be it antlered stag, or grizzly bear.
Sprung from a proud stock of high degree,
As long as a laird's pedigree,
That on many fields have won renown,
He's not the dog that will let you down.
Again and again he's proved his worth
When a badger and fox have gone to earth.
He's won a warm corner in your heart
That nothing but death shall ever part.
Never was truer and stauncher friend
And he will be loyal to the end.
For auld lang syne, may you not forget
When he is old, and his sun has set.

W. Williams

Ch. Reanda King's Ransom photographed by Missy Yuhl.

Epilogue

Considerable research went into the writing of this book and as the chapters grew in length, I became more aware of the tremendous amount of work that individuals have done, not only for our breed, but for the sport of dogs in general. Without these individuals the world of dogs would not be the same.

The newcomer often does not realize what makes a breed, a breeder or a breed club. The breeders who were mentioned in this book did not "make it" in a year, two years or even five years. It took years of breeding to establish a line, and it took years of being a foot soldier to become well known in the breed. Those who have made it and who have a kennel name that is recognized as producing winning dogs have been the individuals who have stuck with it through the lean years and the good years, through the years of some great winners and the years when the wins were not so great. Meanwhile, these individuals worked for the breed, belonged to their all-breed clubs, carried the coffee pots to the matches and stood all day in the rain to ring-steward.

The true dog person is knowledgeable about other breeds and often judges matches for other breed clubs. The true fancier will give of his time—and often money—to the national club and to the local Scottish Terrier club. He will serve on the committees, attend meetings and do the grubby work that it sometimes seems no one else wants to do. He will help new individuals with grooming and handling and he will be pleased when a Scottish Terrier goes best in show, even if it isn't of his own breeding.

The old-timers of the breed, those who have been around for 20, 30 and 40 years, understand this. They have paid their dues and continue to pay them, with few complaints. And this is what makes a great dog person.

Breed and show your dogs, but also get active in your all-breed club and your local Scottish Terrier club. Learn as much as you can about other breeds and about how a dog show functions. And remember, you can't learn it in a day and you don't become a star in a year. But stay with it and you will gain knowledge, make friends and have enough good times for a lifetime.

National Specialty Winners

Date	Best of Breed	Sex	Owner
May 1910	Walescott Invader	(D)	Walescott Kennels
June 1915	Ch. Clonmel Braw Laddie	(D)	A.H. Stewart
June 1916	Ch. Bapton Beatrice	(B)	Miss J. B. Crawford
June 1917	Walescott Albourne Crow	(D)	Walescott Kennels
February 1922	Rannoch Moor Cricket	(D)	Rannoch Moor Kennels
February 1923	Fairwold Plaid	(B)	Fairwold Kennels
February 1924	Fairwold Orsnay Bill	(D)	Fairwold Kennels
February 1925	Allscot Bellstane Blossom	(B)	Dr. N. D. Harvey
February 1926	Allscot Bellstane Blossom	(B)	Dr. N. D. Harvey
February 1927	Albourne Vindicated of Bentley	(D)	Mine Brook Kennels
May 1929	Ornsay Autocrat	(D)	H. D. Bixby
May 1930	Wotan's Watchman	(D)	Monagh Lea Kennels
February 1931	Ch. Ballantrae Wendy	(B)	Mr. and Mrs. C. Barrie
June 1931	Bogelbraie Plutocrat	(D)	Bogelbrae Kennels
February 1932	Heather Aristocrat of Hitofa	(D)	F. Spiekerman
June 1932	Diehard Faith	(B)	Scotsward Kennels
February 1933	Ch. Heather Reveller of Sporan	(D)	S.S. Van Dine
June 1933	Scotsward Jewel	(B)	Mrs. C. B. Ward
February 1934	Ch. Ortley Patience of Hollybourne	(B)	S. L. Froelich
June 1934	Quince Hill Lauder	(D)	Mr. and Mrs. M. Stinemetz
February 1935	Cedar Pond Charmer	(D)	J. Goudie
May 1935	Ch. Heather Reveller of Sporan	(D)	W. Prentice
February 1936	Ch. Goldfinder's Lillie	(B)	E. F. Maloney
May 1936	Ch. Cedar Pond Charmer	(D)	J. Goudie
February 1937	Ch. Glenafton Tamara	(B)	Glen Afton Kennels
May 1937	Marlu Milady	(B)	Marlu Farm Kennels
February 1938	Ch. Marlu Milady	(B)	Marlu Farm Kennels
May 1938	Ch. Cedar Pond Charmer	(D)	J. Goudie
February 1939	Ch. Barberry Knowe Kiltie	(B)	Mr. and Mrs. Charles C. Stalter
May 1939	Ch. Barberry Knowe Kiltie	(B)	Mr. and Mrs. Charles C. Stalter
February 1940	Ch. Shielings Stylist	(D)	Mr. and Mrs. T.H. Snethen
May 1940	Walsing Warrant of Marlu	(D)	Marlu Kennels
February 1941	Relgalf Ribbon Raider	(D)	Relgalf Farm Kennels
May 1941	Ch. Heather Criterion	(D)	E. F. Maloney
February 1942	Ch. Barberry Knowe Larkspur	(B)	Mr. and Mrs. Charles C. Stalter
June 1942	Ch. Relgalf Ribbon Raider	(D)	Relgalf Kennels
February 1943	Fashion Favorite	(B)	Mr. and Mrs. H.D. Israel

June 1943	Ch. Marlu Crusader	(D)	Marlu Farm Kennels
February 1944	Edgerstoune Spitfire	(D)	Mrs. James G. Winan
June 1944	Ch. Ayerscot Anita	(B)	Mr. and Mrs. A. C. Ayers
February 1945	Heather Commodore of Edgerstoune	(D)	Mrs. James G. Winant
September 1945	Ch. Relgalf Rebel Leader	(D)	Relgalf Kennels
February 1946	Ch. Deephaven Warspite	(D)	Marlu Farm Kennels
June 1946	Ch. Deephaven Warspite	(D)	Marlu Farm Kennels
February 1947	Ch. Relgalf Rebel Leader	(D)	Relgalf Kennels
May 1947	Ch. Deephaven Warspite	(D)	Marlu Farm Kennels
February 1948	Ch. Deephaven Warspite	(D)	Marlu Farm Kennels
May 1948	Ch. Deephaven Warspite	(D)	Marlu Farm Kennels
February 1949	Ch. Independent Ben	(D)	J. W. Kelly
May 1949	Ch. Walsing Winning Trick of Edgerstoune	(D)	Mrs. James G. Winant
February 1950	Ch. Walsing Winning Trick of Edgerstoune	(D)	Mrs. James G. Winant
September 1950	Ch. Barberry Knowe Barbican	(D)	Mr. and Mrs. Charles C. Stalter
February 1951	Ch. Barberry Knowe Barbican	(D)	Mr. and Mrs. Charles C. Stalter
May 1951	Ch. Barberry Knowe Barbican	(D)	Mr. and Mrs. Charles C. Stalter
February 1952	Ch. Goldfinder's Admiral	(D)	E.F. Maloney
September 1952	Shieling's Keynoter	(D)	Mr. and Mrs. T. H. Snethen
February 1953	Marlu Clincher	(D)	Paisley Hill Kennels
September 1953	Blanart Bingle of Greenvail	(D)	Mrs. B. G. Vail
February 1954	Rebel Invader	(D)	Mrs. Olive M. Carter
September 1954	Ch. Edgerstoune Troubadour	(D)	Dr. and Mrs. W. S. Carter
February 1955	Ch. Rebel Invader	(D)	Mrs. Olive M. Carter
April 1955	Ch. Rebel Invader	(D)	Mrs. Olive M. Carter
February 1956	Ch. Barberry Knowe Wyndola	(B)	Mr. and Mrs. Charles C. Stalter
May 1956	Fulluvit Festive Fling	(D)	CyAnn Kennels
February 1957	Ch. Cantie Confident	(D)	M.J. Fuller
May 1957	Ch. Barberry Knowe Wager	(D)	Mr. and Mrs. Charles C. Stalter
February 1958	Ch. Janes Grey Wonder	(B)	Mrs. L. Godchaux
September 1958	Ch. Blanart Bewitching	(B)	Mrs. Blanche E. Reeg
February 1959	Reanda Rheola	(B)	Mr. and Mrs. T.H. Snethen
September 1959	Ch. Blanart Bewitching	(B)	Mrs. Blanche E. Reeg

February 1960	Ch. Blanart Bewitching	(B)	Mrs. Blanche E. Reeg
October 1960	Ch. Blanart Bewitching	(B)	Mrs. Blanche E. Reeg
February 1961	Ch. Blanart Bewitching	(B)	Mrs. Blanche E. Reeg
October 1961	Carmichael's Fanfare	(B)	Mrs. Ruth C. Johnson
February 1962	Ch. Walsing Wild Winter of Barberry Knowe	(D)	Mr. and Mrs. Charles C. Stalter
October 1962	Gaidoune Great Bear	(D)	Miss Helen B. Gaither
February 1963	Ch. Carmichael's Fanfare	(B)	Mr. and Mrs. Charles C. Stalter
October 1963	Ch. Carmichael's Fanfare	(B)	Mr. and Mrs. Charles C. Stalter
February 1964	Ch. Carmichael's Fanfare	(B)	Mr. and Mrs. Charles C. Stalter
October 1964	Ch. Carmichael's Fanfare	(B)	Mr. and Mrs. Charles C. Stalter
February 1965	Ch. Gaidoune Grin and Bear It	(D)	Miss Helen B. Gaither
May 1965	Ch. Anstamm Dark Paragon	(B)	Mr. and Mrs. Anthony Stamm
October 1965	Blanart Betwixt	(B)	Miss Cornelia M. Crissey
February 1966	Ch. Gaidoune Grin and Bear It	(D)	Miss Helen B. Gaither
July 1966	Ch. Bardene Bingo	(D)	Mr. E.H. Stuart
October 1966	Ch. Raab Hill Merry Quite Contrary	(B)	Mr. and Mrs. R. A. Marshall
February 1967	Ch. Bardene Bingo	(D)	Mr. E. H. Stuart
May 1967	Ch. Raab Hill Merry Quite Contrary	(B)	Mr. and Mrs. R. A. Marshall
October 1967	Ch. Revran Reprise	(B)	Louise Cedarstrom and Constance Swatsley
February 1968	Ch. Revran Reprise	(B)	Louise Cedarstrom and Constance Swatsley
April 1968	Ch. Carnation Casino	(D)	Carnation Farm Kennels
October 1968	Ch. Barberry Knowe Conductor	(D)	Mrs. Charles C. Stalter
February 1969	Ch. Kirk Nor Outrider	(D)	Mrs. Judtih K. Bonaluto
June 1969	Ch. Gaidoune A Go Go Bear	(B)	Miss Helen B. Gaither
October 1969	Ch. Reanda Rampetta	(B)	Miss Bergit Zakscheloski
February 1970	Ch. Rantin Robin of Lakelynn	(D)	Miss Helen B. Gaither
June 1970	Ch. Charves Dazzler Dyke	(D)	Mr. and Mrs. Robert Charves

October 1970	Ch. Balachan Naughty Gal	(B)	Mrs. Charles C. Stalter
April 1971	Ch. Seagrave's Rogue's Image	(D)	Miss Helen M. Harbulak
October 1971	Ch. Balachan Naughty Gal	(B)	Mrs. Charles C. Stalter
February 1972	Ch. Balachan Naughty Gal	(B)	Mrs. Charles C. Stalter
June 1972	Ch. Bardene Blue McBain	(D)	Wesley L. Slease
October 1972	Ch. Balachan Naughty Gal	(B)	Mrs. Charles C. Stalter
February 1973	Ch. Anstamm Happy Venture	(D)	Mr. and Mrs. Anthony Stamm
October 1973	Ch. Schwer's Dynamic Happy Boy	(D)	Jeanne M. Garlock
March 1974	Ch. Burbury's Sir Lancelot	(D)	Linda L. Catlin
October 1974	Ch. Seagrave's Rogue's Image	(D)	Helen M. Harbulak
April 1975	Ch. Viewpark Versatile	(D)	Jack and Patricia Snyder
October 1975	Dunbar's Democrat of Sandoone	(D)	Richard Hensel
June 1976	Ch. Clanronald's Watch My Smoke	(D)	Mr. and Mrs. William Bowers
October 1976	Ch. Dunbar's Democrat of Sandoone	D)	Richard Hensel and William Crouse
April 1977	Ch. Dunbar's Democrat of Sandoone	(D)	Richard Hensel and William Crouse
October 1977	Ch. Anstamm Happy Sonata	(B)	Miriam Stamm
March 1978	Ch. Anstamm Happy Sonata	(B)	Miriam Stamm
October 1978	Ch. Dunbar's Democrat of Sandoone	(D)	Richard Hensel and William Crouse
June 1979	Ch. Sandgreg's Headliner	(D)	William McGinnes and Barbara DeSaye
October 1979	Ch. Schaeffer's Calling Card	(D)	Joan G. Damon
June 1980	Ch. Democratic Victory	(D)	Robert L. Willis
October 1980	Ch. Democratic Victory	(D)	Robert L. Willis
June 1981	Ch. Braeburn's Close Encounter	(B)	Mr. and Mrs. William R. McGinnis
October 1981	Ch. Democratic Victory	(D)	Barbara A. and Robert L. Willis
June 1982	Ch. Democratic Victory	(D)	Barbara A. and Robert L. Willis
October 1982	Anstamm All American	(D)	Christen Helper
May 1983	Ch. Ashmoor at the Ritz	(B)	Robert V. Moore, III
October 1983	Ch. Jabberwok Here Comes the Sun	(D)	Merle and Carolyn Taylor
April 1984	Ch. Perlor Playboy	(D)	Elizabeth Cooper
October 1984	Ch. Braeburn's Close Encounter	(B)	Sonnie and Alan Novick

April 1985	Ch. Hughcrest Sparklin' Burgundy	(B)	Chris and Judy Hughes
October 1985	Ch. Hughcrest Bottoms Up	(B)	Christine and Michael Cook
February 1986	Ch. Sandgreg's Foxmoor	(D)	Mark George
October 1986	Hughcrest Daiquiri Doll	(B)	Chris and Judy Hughes
March 1987	Ch. Simonsez Charlie the Charmer	(D)	E. Louise Simon and Frances Moore
October 1987	Ch. Deblin's Back Talk	(D)	Deborah McGrory and Lynn Struck
May 1988	Sandgreg's Foxmoor	(D)	Dr. James and Eliza Boso
October 1988	Anstamm Heat Wave	(B)	Anstamm Kennels
June 1989	Ch. Anstamm Heat Wave	(B)	Anstamm Kennels
October 1989	Ch. Sandgreg's Foxmoor	(D)	Dr. James and Elizabeth Boso
April 1990	Ch. Anstamm Heat Wave	(B)	Anstamm Kennels
October 1990	Ch. Brookhill's Morning Edition	(B)	Marjorie Carpenter
June 1991	Ch. Brookhill's Morning Edition	(B)	Marjorie Carpenter
October 1991	Ch. Brookhill's Morning Edition	(B)	Marjorie Carpenter
April 1992	Ch. Hopscotch Head's We Win	(B)	Marg Moran McQuinn
October 1992	Ch. Hopscotch Head's We Win	(B)	Marg Moran McQuinn
April 1993	Ch. Gaelforce Post Script	(B)	Vandra Huber
October 1993	Ch. Gaelforce Post Script	(B)	Vandra Huber
March 1994	Ch. Gaelforce Post Script	(B)	Vandra Huber and Dr. Joe Kinnerne

Annual Awards of the STCA

There are a variety of awards presented through the Scottish Terrier Club of America and they are donated by various members. Specific information for the awards may be obtained by writing to the Recording Secretary.

The Frances G. Lloyd Memorial Trophy is the only perpetual trophy awarded and is considered to be the club's most prestigious award. This cup was first awarded in 1921 and is awarded to the dog or bitch scoring the greatest number of points for Best of Breed based on the championship point rating of the breed. The winner's name is engraved on the trophy, which remains in the custody of the STCA. This cup is exhibited at the annual meeting in October.

The Gilwyn Best of Opposite Sex Trophy awarded to the dog or bitch winning the most points for Best of Opposite Sex.

The McVan All-Breed Award is awarded for Best of Breed wins with a different count tally than the Lloyd Trophy.

The McArthur Bred by Exhibitor Trophy awarded to the exhibitor accumulating the most points with either a dog or a bitch in the bred by exhibitor class.

The Anstruthers American bred Award is awarded to the exhibitor accumulating the most points in the American bred dog classes.

The Am Anger Cinderella Memorial Trophy awarded to the exhibitor accumulating the most points in the American bred bitch classes.

The Champion Duff-De Packman Award goes to the exhibitor accumulating the most points in the puppy dog classes.

The Bar None Puppy Bitch Award awarded to the exhibitor accumulating the most points in the puppy bitch classes.

The Ch. Sandgreg's Editorial Stud Dog Award is awarded to the owner of the dog siring the greatest number of Scottish Terrier champions during the year.

The Champion Lad Alberta Memorial Trophy awarded to the owner of the bitch producing the greatest number of Scottish Terrier champions during the year.

The Mr. and Mrs. Charles C. Stalter Trophy offered to Best of Breed at Montgomery County Specialty Show.

The Hughcrest Trophy awarded for Best of Winners at Montgomery County Specialty Show.

The Louise Ellsworth Memorial Trophy awarded for Best of Opposite Sex at Montgomery County Specialty Show.

The Bernice Ayers Trophy awarded to Best in Sweepstakes winner at the fall specialty.

In order to qualify for any of these annual awards the owner and all co-owners must be members in good standing of the STCA at the time of the win.

Points for the awards are calculated for the calendar year as published in the AKC *Gazette*. The winners and runners-up are listed in the *Bagpiper* and the annual awards are presented in October at the annual meeting.

In addition to the above awards, the following are also offered:

The Lochnel Junior Showmanship Award for the junior handler who achieves the most number of wins while handling a Scottish Terrier during any given period.

Breeder's Cup Trophy awarded to the breeder of the Lloyd Trophy winner.

The following awards are also given by the STCA:

The Anstamm Achievement Award for outstanding service to the club or for notable achievement or meritorious accomplishments affecting or relating to the Scottish Terrier.

The Sterling Silver Medallion Award is awarded to members who have rendered outstanding service to the Club.

The Anthony Stamm Veterinary Memorial Fund. The STCA will donate $100 annually to a college or university in memory of STCA members who died during the preceding year.

Gaines Good Sportsmanship Medal is given by Gaines Dog Food to honor a person who has worked behind-the-scenes, giving unselfishly of his or her time and talents for the STCA.

1947 Breed Standard

SKULL—(5 Points): Long, of medium width, slightly domed, and covered with short hard hair. It should not be quite flat, as there should be a slight stop or drop between the eyes.

(1) MUZZLE—(5 Points): In proportion to the length of skull, with not too much taper toward the nose. Nose should be black and of good size. The jaws should be level and square. The nose projects somewhat over the mouth, giving the impression that the upper jaw is longer than the lower. The teeth should be evenly placed, having a scissors or level bite, with the former being preferable.

EYES—(5 Points): Set wide apart, small and of almond shape, not round. Color to be dark brown or nearly black. To be bright, piercing and set well under the brow.

EARS—(10 Points): Small, prick, set well up on the skull, rather pointed but not cut. The hair on them should be short and velvety.

NECK—(5 Points): Moderately short, thick, and muscular, strongly set on sloping shoulders, but not so short as to appear clumsy.

CHEST—(5 Points): Broad and very deep, well let down between the fore legs.

BODY—(15 Points): Moderately short and well ribbed up with strong loin, deep flanks and very muscular hindquarters.

(2) LEGS AND FEET—(10 Points): Both fore and hind legs should be short and very heavy in bone in proportion to the size of the dog. Fore legs straight or slightly bent with elbows close to the body. Scottish Terriers should not be out at the elbows. Stifles should be well bent and legs straight from hock to heel. Thighs very muscular. Feet round and thick with strong nails, fore feet larger than the hind feet.

NOTE: The gait of the Scottish Terrier is peculiarly its own and is very characteristic of the breed. It is not the square trot or walk that is desirable in the long-legged breeds. The fore legs do not move in exact parallel planes—rather in reaching out incline slightly inward. This is due to the shortness of leg and width of chest. The action of the rear legs should be square and true and at the trot both the hocks and stifles should be flexed with a vigorous motion.

TAIL—(2½ Points): Never cut and about seven inches long, carried with a slight curve but not over the back.

COAT—(15 Points): Rather short, about two inches, dense undercoat with outer coat intensely hard and wiry.

(3) SIZE AND WEIGHT—(10 Points): Equal consideration must be given to height, length of back and weight. Height at shoulder for either sex should be about 10 inches. Generally, a well balanced Scottish Terrier dog of correct size should weigh from 19 to 22 lbs. and a bitch from 18 to 21 lbs. The principal objective must be symmetry and balance.

COLOR—(2½ Points): Steel or iron grey, brindle or grizzled, black, sandy or wheaten. White markings are objectionable and can be allowed only on the chest and that to a slight extent only.

GENERAL APPEARANCE—(10 Points): The face should wear a keen sharp and active expression. Both head and tail should be carried well up. The dog should look very compact, well muscled and powerful, giving the impression of immense power in a small size.

(4) PENALTIES—Soft coat, round or very light eye, over or undershot jaw, obviously over or under size, shyness, timidity or failure to show with head and tail up are faults to be penalized. No judge should put to Winners or Best of Breed any Scottish Terrier not showing real Terrier character in the ring.

SCALE OF POINTS

Skull	5	Legs and Feet	10
Muzzle	5	Tail	2½
Eyes	5	Coat	15
Ears	10	Size	10
Neck	5	Color	2½
Chest	5	Appearance	10
Body	15	Total	100 Pts.

Books about the Scottish Terrier

Ash, Edward C., *The Scottish Terrier*, Cassell and Company, Ltd., London, 1936.

Bruette, Dr. William, *Scottish Terrier*, G. Howard Watt, New York, 1934.

Buckley, Holland, *The Scottish Terrier*, The Illustrated News Company, Ltd., London, 1913.

Caspersz, Dorothy S., *The Scottish Terrier Handbook*, Nicholson and Watson, London, 1951.

—————., *The Popular Scottish Terrier*, Arco Publishing Company, Inc., New York, 1962.

Davies, C.J., *The Scottish Terrier*, Everett and Company, London.

Ewing, Fayette C., *The Book of the Scottish Terrier*, Orange Judd Publishing Company, Inc., 1936.

Gannon, Robert, *How to Raise and Train a Scottish Terrier*, T.F.H. Publications, Inc., New Jersey, 1955, 1960.

Haynes, William, *Scottish and Irish Terriers*, The MacMillan Company, New York, 1925.

Johns, Rowland, *Our Friend the Scottish Terrier*, E.P. Dutton and Company, Inc., New York, 1933.

Kirk, T. Allen, Jr., MD, *This is the Scottish Terrier*, T.F.H. Publications, Inc., New Jersey, 1971.

Lee, Muriel P., *The Whelping and Rearing of Puppies*, Plantin Press, Minnesota, 1984.

Marvin, John T. *The Complete Scottish Terrier*, Howell Book House, New York, 1971.

Mountjoy, T.W. Hancock, *Points of the Dog*, Eveleigh Nash and Grayson, London, 1930.

Penn-Bull, Betty, *The Kennelgarth Scottish Terrier Book*, Saiga Publishing Company, Ltd., Surrey, England, 1983.

Scottish Terrier Club of America Yearbook: 1932, 1939, 1948, 19671, 1965, 1974, 1986, 1991.

Snethen, Mr. and Mrs. T.H., *Pet Scottish Terrier*, All-Pets Books, Inc.

Terrier Type, Volume 27, No. 8, July 1988.

Index

Page numbers in **boldface** refer to illustrations. For the user's convenience, all titles have been removed from dogs' names.

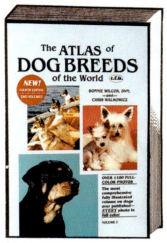

H-1091, 912 pp
over 1100 color photos

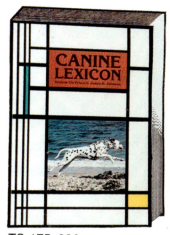

TS-175, 896 pp
over 1300 color photos

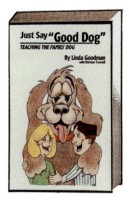

TS-204, 160 pp
over 50 line drawings

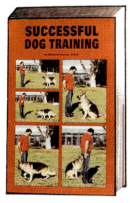

TS-205, 156 pp
over 130 color photos

H-1106, 544pp
over 400 color photos

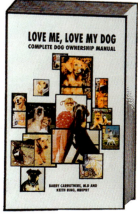

TS-212, 256 pp
over 140 color photos

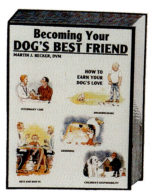

TS-220, 64 pp
over 50 color illus.

223

PS-872, 240 pp
178 color illus.

H-1095, 272 pp
over 160 color illus.

KW-227, 96 pp
100 color photos

H-1016, 224 pp
135 photos

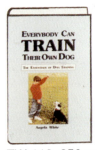
TW-113, 256 pp
200 color photos

H-962, 255 pp
nearly 100 photos

PS-607, 254 pp
136 B & W photos

TS-101, 192 pp
over 100 photos

TW-102, 256 pp
over 200 color photos

SK-044, 64 pp
over 50 color
photos

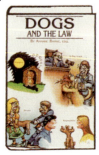
TS-130, 160 pp
50 color illus.

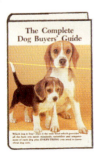
H-1061, 608 pp
100 B & W photos

H-969, 224 pp
62 color photos